SOUL
Dating to
SOUL
Mating

SOUL
Dating to
SOUL
Mating

On the Path Toward Spiritual Partnership

BASHA KAPLAN, PSY.D., AND GAIL PRINCE, M.ED.

FOREWORD BY CAROLINE MYSS, PH.D.

A Perigee Book

A Perigee Book
Published by The Berkley Publishing Group
A member of Penguin Putnam Inc.
375 Hudson Street
New York, New York 10014

First edition: February 1999

Published simultaneously in Canada.

The Penguin Putnam Inc. World Wide Web site address is
http://www.penguinputnam.com

Library of Congress Cataloging-in-Publication Data

Kaplan, Basha.
    Soul dating to soul mating : on the path toward spiritual partnership / Basha Kaplan and Gail
Prince ; foreword by Caroline Myss. — 1st ed.
        p.   cm.
    "A Perigee book."
    Includes bibliographical references.
    ISBN 0-399-52476-2
    1. Mate selection—United States.   2. Soul mates—United States.   3. Dating (Social customs)—
United States.   4. Spiritual life.
    I. Prince, Gail.   II. Title.
    HQ801.K35   1999
    646.7'7—dc21   98-45969
                                                                                      CIP

Printed in the United States of America

10 9 8 7 6 5 4 3 2 1

TO JEFF.

Basha's loving husband and spiritual partner, and Gail's mentor and dear friend, who supported us emotionally and spiritually throughout the writing of this book.

As producer and codirector, his collaboration in creating this book has added substance and dimension. Without his friendship, insight, and tenacity, this book would never have happened.

BASHA'S DEDICATION

To my mother, Ruth Blumenthal, and to the memory of my father, Jack Blumenthal, with love, gratitude, and appreciation for all the lessons they taught me.

GAIL'S DEDICATION

To my two sets of parents, Louis and Reba Geisman and Uncle Milton and Aunt Libby Schwartz, whose loving and respectful relationships served as positive role models.

Contents

Foreword
Caroline Myss, Ph.D.

Everyone dreams about finding the "perfect" mate. My workshops are filled with individuals in search of a partner with whom they can share their lives. When I ask people, "How many of you women were told when you were growing up that someday your prince would come?" invariably all hands rise along with smirks of disappointment. And when I quiz the men with, "How many of you are holding on to the myth that someday that perfect woman would come along who would always be an ageless beauty?" laughingly, most shrug their shoulders as if to say, "Well, can you blame me? That's what all men are looking for."

The next logical question is, "And how many of you have succeeded in this quest?" At this point, usually all of the audience members break into laughter, only it isn't really all that humorous. Many—indeed most of them—come from battle-scarred relationships that failed for various reasons. Some report that their mates cheated on them (one of the more popular reasons for a divorce), others describe a marriage in which their partners simply could not pursue a spiritual path alongside them, and many comment that their marriage lacked any depth of genuine communication. They knew that they were in a marriage of convenience as opposed to a marriage of love and that they simply could no longer live that way. Regardless of the particulars, the core of each reason was essentially the same: The person they married was not the person they thought he or she was prior to getting married, and the institution of marriage along with all the romantic perfection it was supposed to ensure was an illusion.

Nevertheless, in spite of all the reports from the survivors of these broken marriages, and amid all of the social studies that suggest we are a society moving too rapidly to create genuinely stable romantic bonds with another person, we remain determined to try. And we should.

We humans are deeply romantic creatures. How can it be otherwise? We thrive on the energy of love. Our bodies require love for health and our hearts for tranquility. Let's face it, we were all brought up on fantasy tales that tell us that life has the potential to offer us romantic fulfillment if we can only find that one person who is our "other half," a term that in and of itself suggests that we are essentially imbalanced until we find that certain someone.

The crucial question is, Can we really achieve the quality of relationship that we are seeking, and if so, how in the world do we attain it? Pursuing this question and offering rich directives toward helping people create a devoted and loving relationship in their lives is the goal of this wonderful book by Basha Kaplan, Psy.D., and Gail Prince, M.Ed.

Basha and Gail have combined their expertise as counselors in this text, sharing their personal experiences as women in search of a partnership—a soul mate—along with the stories of many of their clients as a means of guiding others toward understanding what it takes first to identify a right partner and then to do the necessary groundwork to maximize its success.

Toward that goal, Basha and Gail have included a series of questions for self-examination as they discuss the issues that one needs to pursue in order to evaluate one's own vulnerabilities in relationships. It is crucial for each person to recognize his or her reasons for being drawn to certain "types" of people, for instance, and it is equally important for people to investigate their own patterns in approaching relationships. Do you fall in love before even really knowing the person? Do you project your fantasy mate onto this other person without realizing that you are doing it? Do you immediately think in terms of marriage on a first date with someone?

These types of questions are pathways into ourselves that give us insights into our own motives and vulnerabilities. We need to know the answers to these questions and the numerous others presented in this wonderful book in order to become more conscious of our strengths and our weaknesses.

In my own work, I meet so many people who introduce me to their partners and describe him or her (mostly women do this) as a soul mate. When I ask them where they met, many reveal that they met in a support group or right after one of them just experienced a failed relationship. With these types of relationships, a bond forms immediately because of the natural combination of pain-sufferer and rescuer. But as I point out in my workshops, what happens to these types of relationships when one of the two people involved decides to heal? Can the bond withstand the transition to strength? Many cannot, and thus the soul-mate status of these individuals is reduced to just another failed relationship.

What if these two people entered into a relationship with more clarity about who they were and what they needed from a relationship? What if these two people were able to openly explore with each other the question of is it their fear of being alone that is drawing them to each other, or is it a genuine attraction? These are bold questions, to be sure, but deciding to marry a person is one of life's boldest moves and for that reason alone, one should be able to openly discuss such intimate truths about each other. After all, the decision to invest the whole of one's life with another's should not under any circumstance be done under an illusion of perfection because the fact is, there is no such thing as perfection. In admitting that this is the case, we stand all the more chance of creating balance by recognizing and accepting the other person as well as ourselves for the people we really are rather than who we would like them and ourselves to be.

In reading this book, I could not help but rethink a position that I have long held, which is that "soul mate" is just another contemporary romantic term that has been upgraded due to our living in a more spiritual culture. If there is such a thing as soul-mate relationships, then they are going to take work to achieve because the very term implies a desire to partner with each other at a conscious soul level instead of the more traditional social level. The term soul mate indicates that we are seeking a union with a person capable of sharing our divinity and the depth of our interior psyches and spirits. Certainly that goal is not a fantasy, but is the attainment of that goal a fantasy?

I would say it is not, but I would also caution people to understand that should they want this quality of relationship, then they had best be prepared to work more on themselves than on changing their mates. The task in a soul-mate relationship is to discover through a bond with another person not only a devoted and cherished partner, but also one through whom each individual can enter into his or her shadow self in order to bring that part of themselves into the light. What this path of spirituality is all about is how satisfying it is to be able to walk through both our light and shadow with another person.

This is a true soul mate and not a romantic illusion and thus, the romance that exists in a soul-mate relationship is all the more romantic because it is real.

Soul Dating to Soul Mating: On the Path Toward Spiritual Partnership is a delicious guide toward self-preparation for becoming a person capable of achieving a soul mate for a life's partner. It is not a "how do you find that person" book—thank goodness. Rather, it is wonderful text of self-examination—like a soul and psyche makeover—that directs a person into self-discovery of one's own soul in order that it can genuinely be shared with another.

—Caroline M. Myss, Ph.D.

Acknowledgments

BASHA'S ACKNOWLEDGMENTS

I am so grateful to my inspirational and visionary teachers and friends: Dr. Caroline Myss, Dr. Norm Shealy, and Dr. Fernando Flores of Logonet.

I am most thankful for my loving and supportive mother-in-law, Gertrude Kaplan, and my deceased grandparents and uncle, Leah, Meyer, and Sam Meystel, who always believed in me and gave me unconditional love.

To my friends Penny Rotheiser and Karen Kassy, who took time out from their lives to graciously and lovingly share their wisdom, advice, and direction.

During this process, I was especially blessed with my dear friends and colleagues Marvin and Arlene Woods, who joined Jeff and me to create a "spiritual partnership think tank." This allowed me to further create and develop my vision, thoughts, and ideas. Their dedication to this book is an inspiration.

I offer immense appreciation and gratitude for the assistance I received from my higher consciousness and the universe, which inspired me to new horizons and possibilities.

GAIL'S ACKNOWLEDGMENTS

I am most grateful to my significant other, Ed, to David, my son and soul mate, and to my friends who supported and encouraged me through the writing of this book.

To Bruce Wexler for his creativity, patience, and dedication.

OUR ACKNOWLEDGMENTS

We give special thanks to all our clients, support group members, and workshop participants who so openly and trustingly shared their fears, struggles, hopes, and dreams, and from whom we continue to learn as we travel together on the path;

To America Martinez, our spiritual advisor and friend, for her wisdom, guidance, and support throughout the process;

To Damaris Rowland, our agent and friend, for believing in us and recognizing our unique message;

To our editor, Sheila Curry, and all the professional staff at Perigee/Berkley for taking a chance, and helping us in so many ways. Your enthusiasm has helped make this book a reality.

We also want to include in this group all our former dates and mates, whose contribution to our lives is greatly appreciated.

Introduction and Philosophy

Basha and Gail have invented a new dating model to help individuals find a soulful connection in their dating and mating lives. Many of today's books focus on keeping romance and passion alive or on how to get married. Our book is different. It teaches people how to find the perfect partner for them so that the relationship grows stronger and better every day. No more power struggles!

Many men and women are struggling with finding fulfilling, committed relationships. The divorce rate is soaring yet people still strive to connect through marriage. Originally, marriage was designed to provide economic security, safety, and comfort and to satisfy the social needs of families, religious institutions, and communities. Graphically, traditional marriage may look like this:

$$WE = I + I.$$ The WE equals the
Individual plus the Individual.

Each person has a separate life; the relationship comprises two separate I's.

Or the marriage may look like this:

$$WE = I + i.$$

In this relationship, the partnership is not equal. One of the I's takes the other's identity or gives up a large part of him- or herself to make the partnership work.

In a traditional marriage the goal was to maintain the status quo. Loving relationships were sustained by focusing on looking out for #1 and viewing others as vehicles to satisfy our personal needs. Traditional roles dictated that the woman stayed home and took care of the house and family while the man was the breadwinner. Additionally, men and women could depend on staying married to the same person throughout their lives, holding on to the same job to retirement, maintaining clearly defined gender roles, and having a nuclear family that lived in close proximity. In essence, life felt relatively safe, secure, and insular.

Beginning in the '60s with the Women's Movement, the world has been rapidly transforming. The developments that have affected our relationships include unstable economics which force more women into the workforce, and allows other women the ability to choose to work. These are the result of renegotiated relationships, decreased job security for men, shake-up of gender roles, new ways of communicating on a global information highway, high divorce rates, and the dissemination of psychological and spiritual ideas within the last ten years through books, TV, and news talk shows. In addition, home computers in our culture offer different possibilities and ideas related to communications, relationships, and work.

This lack of security and constant change in every area of our lives makes many yearn for a relationship that will endure. There is a growing consciousness for many of us that we want and *need* more—more than our parents' traditional unions—more meaningfulness in our lives and in our relationships. Much more is *needed* and demanded in a marriage today. More than ever we are trying to get love right. To achieve this, we are required to use a different set of values in seeking a partner. Less value should be put on the concrete components, and more emphasis on spiritual meaningfulness, connectedness, shared values, and intimacy. Divorce is symptomatic of a profound loss of vision concerning life and love.

A relationship can be a vehicle for self-discovery and awakening. However, love is not enough. Partners must to be best friends to rely on each other for all of their needs: emotional, psychological, spiritual, and physical. In an ideal relationship, partners work as a team to satisfy each other's needs, uplift one another, and journey together toward personal growth and sexual and spiritual fulfillment. Soul mates and spiritual partnerships are essential for answering these deeper needs, part of which is to make the world a more humane place.

We were inspired to write this book because thousands of people who have gone through our workshops have gotten great results. Although we will be focusing on soul mate relationships, the information presented throughout this book is equally applicable to leading a fulfilling traditional relationship—what we call companionship.

Soul mates touch each other at the heart and soul level. When they are with their partner, they feel as if they've come home to themselves. Soul mates provide a safe and nurturing haven for their partner to work through their past wounds by communicating with each other in healthy and nurturing ways. To achieve these goals, the focus of the relationship is on authenticity, intimacy, and unconditional love.

Soul mates are consciously aware that emotional and spiritual growth is a driving force in their lives, both as a couple and individually. They are learning to trust and listen to their higher self. Soul mates acknowledge that they are in each other's lives to learn lessons. There are no guarantees that the partnership will last forever. Partners remain together as long as they both continue to learn and grow as individuals as well as a couple.

We will also be introducing the reader to the type of relationship called *spiritual partnership*. This is a life partnership to which we all can aspire. Spiritual partners know that their union is beyond the ordinary, that it transcends the normal level of consciousness, and that divine intervention guided them toward each other when the time was right. Partners are brought together because they have been rewarded for their courage in doing an enormous amount of emotional, psychological, and spiritual healing.

When you are in the presence of spiritual partners, their interaction seems magical. Because they have accomplished so much personal growth, the focus of their relationship is on contribution and service. Spiritual partners understand that everything happens for a reason and are at peace knowing that they can contend with whatever life presents.

A graphic representation of spiritual partnership looks like this:

I WE I

In order to achieve the "we," each person must be a complete "I," a clearly defined individual. Each "I" must attain a state of relative wholeness, know and feel comfortable with all parts of him- or herself, feel fulfilled inside, and be capable of happily living alone. In other words, to want a relationship, not need one.

The two "I's" remain while creating at the same time a new "we." This requires inventing a new way to live, "doing" and "being" together each day. For love to endure, each couple must share similar spiritual and philosophical vision and complementary values in their lives. They commit to the full development of themselves as individuals and as partners. The emphasis in their relationship is on acceptance, friendship, romance, communication, and unconditional love. Being on the path to soul mate or spiritual partnership entails a change in consciousness and a transformation of one's relationship to self and life. The total self must be a participant rather than an observer.

Being *on the path* is the process that directs us to discover who we really are; to find the fulfillment, purpose, and sense of meaning that is missing in our lives. It is a journey that integrates the spiritual elements with the worldly. It is the beginning of an ongoing commitment to look inward for answers. With practical, hands-on psychological, spiritual, and cognitive explanations and homework assignments, each reader can feel hopeful and competent to journey on the path to self-discovery. The ultimate goal is achieving a sacred union with one's partner. We need a new consciousness, a new set of distinctions and techniques with concurrent skills to achieve this end.

Our method is as follows: The *Seven Spiritual Wisdoms* are the foundation of this book. They are the basic tenets of living a full life as well as the prerequisites for building a spiritual union with another. The Seven Spiritual Wisdoms present a new way of looking at life by helping you clarify your values and beliefs, stimulating you intellectually and emotionally, and encouraging you to discover who you really are *before* you enter into a soul partnership. They also help you reflect on how your spirituality (personal connection to God and the universe) manifests itself in your everyday life. This will help you understand the world in ways that facilitate your journey through it, which makes the process of soul dating and soul mating easier.

We need to understand and use the Seven Spiritual Wisdoms as we travel through the relationship process. They must be lived before, during, and after the dating and mating journey. Consider the following sequential stages in seeking and maintaining a soul mate or spiritual partnership:

1. Soulwork, or Inner Preparation: Building the Intrapersonal Relationship
2. Soul Dating, or Dating with Consciousness
3. The Partner—Is This the One?
4. Marriage
5. Throughout the Marriage

Since this book concerns finding a soul mate, the first two of these stages will be explored in depth following full discussion of the Seven Spiritual Wisdoms.

Stage 1: Soulwork—The soul is that part of us that transcends the five senses. It is part of a magical realm, not apparent to our everyday eyes. The soul comprises the intuitive and feeling parts of our nature when they are connected beyond our personality to our higher self. The soul experiences our divine nature and energy and allows us to go beyond the explainable levels of our conscious mind. This connection to God and the universe characterizes our spirituality, which is the essence of our soul. The soul lives by the universal law that each of us travels a unique path which involves growth and learning lessons.

Soulwork is the journey of integrating our soul and personality; it shifts our attention from viewing the world in front of our eyes to viewing it from the inside, through our new consciousness. This is the individualized path to inner healing, meaningfulness, and wholeness. Our inner preparation for a soul mate relationship needs to be individualized in a step-by-step manner, to fully actualize our potential for a soulful partnership. We need to determine the level of work and awareness we must acquire to achieve this goal. Fully engaging in the activities discussed in this book helps us reinvent who we are and guides us to become the person we were meant to be, which leads us to our soul mate.

Stage 2: Soul Dating—Once we know who we are and what is important to us as individuals, dating with consciousness helps us use specific skills to make sure that we really know who our partner is. Most people choose a marriage partner using either their head or their heart to make the decision. In soul dating, we learn to combine our wisdom and our heart in making this decision so that both the "who" and the "what" are supported. This process also involves discovering if our potential partner really supports us and has the same vision for his or her life that we have for ours. The goal is to communicate effectively, which creates and maintains a healthy relationship. It is also important that we find a person who is in the same place as we are and shares similar values. There is no right or wrong, no good or bad; there's just finding the right person. This step-by-step process transforms dating into a journey of self-discovery and healing which ultimately leads to a fulfilling and meaningful soul mate relationship.

Throughout our discussion of both stages, soulwork and soul dating, we break down the sections into steps. After discussing the theme of each step, we include a list of specific questions for you to answer and activities for you to do. We also provide a meditation to close each step.

To achieve the end results, our book includes methods that are cognitive, behavioral, spiritual, and psychological. We primarily focus on consciousness, meaningfulness, and manageability. The themes of consciousness and meaningfulness are emphasized in the Seven Spiritual Wisdoms, while manageability is emphasized during the hands-on steps of soulwork and soul dating.

Consciousness is seeing and admitting the truth about ourselves and others, without illusion, as we journey toward soul mate partnership. Some of the attributes of consciousness are:

⋄ Recognizing that attitude is power
⋄ Knowing who you are
⋄ Taking responsibility for your life rather than be victim to your circumstances
⋄ Choosing new ways of behaving and feeling

Meaningfulness is the deep feeling that life makes sense and is filled with purpose. It's the attitude of looking forward to each day with enthusiasm and gratitude. It's the connection to divine energy which inspires our contribution to the universe. Meaningfulness is essential in order to have a soul connection.

Manageability is planning and directing your life by focusing on responsibility and active participation in inventing your future. Through the individualized hands-on skills and techniques we present in this book, your abilities in this realm will be greatly enhanced. Additionally, we focus on helping each individual connect thoughts and emotions to promote healthy behavior. Together we help you determine the meaning, function, and consequences of your beliefs and how they might sabotage love.

We need to date and mate differently or we'll end up repeating the same mistakes because that's all we know. Anyone can get married. Our goal is helping people discover the essence of who they are and learn to utilize and trust their intuition and higher self to guide them in their search for a partner. Also, working in a psychological, spiritual, and practical framework encourages your inner development and a fuller, more balanced outer life, which prepares you for your soul mate or spiritual partner.

We want this book to be intimate, inspiring, and heartfelt, as well as informational. We will be sharing true stories with you about individuals, including ourselves, who have courageously embraced and lived the Seven Spiritual Wisdoms and the soulwork and soul dating steps.

We feel it is important to let you know us intimately—who we are and how we came to write this book through our personal journeys. Because we are both committed to walking the talk, we want to share some of our personal struggles, both past and present, and how they have influenced our relationships. We are both excellent teachers because we are wounded healers, and we teach by sharing examples of the mistakes we've made and how we learned from them. We want you to be aware that you're not alone on this journey. We've struggled and are still struggling with some of the same issues you may be confronting.

BASHA

I was the firstborn and was raised in a close-knit extended family. I walked at nine months and talked at one year. (People tell me I haven't stopped since.) As a young child, I appeared hyperactive and precocious. I was guided by my intuition, questioning everything I was told. I had a difficult time accepting anyone's rules unless I thought they made sense. I valued truth and open communication, as far back as I can remember.

As loving as my parents tried to be, I never felt totally understood and accepted. Instead of acknowledging my talents and unique abilities, they acted as if my behavior were average. They never congratulated me for my accomplishments, they just focused on how I could improve. My father worked all the time and I rarely saw him. In those days, that's what fathers did to show their love and devotion to their family. When he was around, he hardly ever spoke to me except to point out what I did wrong and to tell me what to do. I deliberately got in trouble so he would pay attention to me. I guess I figured negative attention was better than no attention at all.

My mother, on the other hand, showed her love by giving me lots of attention. However, she would qualify whatever praise she handed out. For example, she would say, "You look wonderful, but . . ." or "You did very well this term but you can do better." Many of my friends and relatives expressed to me that they wished they had parents like mine. This reinforced my belief that I had to keep on improving myself to deserve them, as I never felt O.K. the way I was.

I always felt inner turmoil between expressing myself and getting approval from others. In order to feel that I belonged, I discounted my intuition; it was causing great internal conflict by making it difficult for me to follow my family's and society's norms. While I tried to conform to what others wanted of me, I buried parts of myself. I became a stranger to myself. As a result, I felt "ugly"—even though I was physically attractive and had a vivacious personality. When I was thirteen I developed an eating disorder to compensate for my negative feelings concerning my self-worth, which was tied up with my belief that I had to look good in other people's eyes.

I was a late bloomer in many respects. As a teenager, I dated infrequently. Feeling unattractive and uncertain, I hovered on the outskirts of the "cool" crowd. At twenty I started dating a great deal after observing what successful women daters did and copying their style. I wanted so badly to be loved that when I dated I became a chameleon, ready to become who and what the other person wanted me to be. When I finally felt that the man I was dating really liked me, I would then reveal my true nature. Because it didn't fit with the image I had projected to initiate the relationship, the man would drop me. This reinforced my dual belief that I was unlovable and that men couldn't be trusted, especially with intimate information regarding who I was. Although I placed the blame on my dates, in retrospect I see that I betrayed them, they didn't betray me.

Most of my dates when I was younger weren't kind and nurturing. I was drawn to cool and aloof men who weren't there for me—couldn't be there for me—and I tried to win their love. The more unavailable someone was, the more I was attracted because, as I learned later, I didn't love myself. At twenty-seven, a loving man I felt safe and authentic with became serious and wanted to get married. I rejected him because I didn't feel worthy of his wonderful, nurturing nature.

Growing up, I observed that even though my parents loved each other, they didn't share similar interests and had different values. I frequently observed them in power struggles. Also, from my perspective, they were not emotionally intimate with each other.

To tell the truth, there were very few couples I knew that I would want to trade places with. Most people seemed so unhappy being married. I swore to myself that I wouldn't marry someone if it didn't feel intimately connected and emotionally safe. I knew that in order to accomplish this goal, I first needed to learn to be my own best friend.

When I was twenty-eight I moved to San Diego to attend graduate school for my doctorate in clinical psychology, which was ironic because I had reached a point where my eating disorder was out of control. I was either starving myself or bingeing. I knew in my heart I needed to make some major changes in my life.

I began therapy and started on my inner journey by healing psychologically and reconnecting with my spiritual side through a study of Jung and Existentialism. As part of the process, I entered what is called the Dark Night of the Soul, a valuable part of the journey that many of us experience when life feels overwhelming. Going through this process inspired change and transformation in every area of my life. Even though at times I felt like a stranger, I continued to put myself on the path of self-discovery and couldn't stop learning and growing. (This concept will be discussed in detail later in the book.)

To complement therapy and reading, I also attended numerous workshops and seminars, including Overeaters Anonymous. I became immersed in discovering who I was and rekindled my connection to my higher self and divine energy. My eating disorder started disappearing with this internal focus on healing. This process took many years. In fact, I still maintain diligence concerning binge eating and its connection to losing touch with myself.

I felt like I was reborn, my life had renewed meaning and purpose. I no longer needed anyone to fill me up. I loved who I was and swore that I would never lose myself again. Through this process of learning, self-discovery, and healing, I started creating and living the Seven Spiritual Wisdoms, the foundation of this book. I also became more authentic in my relationships with men. I began dating often, frequently attracting loving, open men.

In 1987, I read Linda Leonard's book *On the Way to the Wedding: Transforming the Love Relationship*. This book became my bible because in it she introduced me to the possibility of a spiritual partnership. I prayed for guidance and trusted my inner voice to teach me the lessons I needed to learn in order to be ready for this higher level of intimacy. This was a difficult process since I had no external role models. Most of the relationships I observed among my family, friends, and clients were companionships, apparently devoid of the soul values I was seeking.

I was now ready to meet my life partner. In 1990, I met Bob. We definitely were soul mates. I grew tremendously in this relationship. The most important lesson was learning how to love unconditionally. We dated off and on for four years. I finally said good-bye, however, realizing we could not evolve into spiritual partners. I wouldn't settle. I never gave up my belief that the divine would lead me to a sacred union, in God's time, if I was true to my path and lived life with purpose and meaning.

Six months after ending my relationship with Bob, my father died suddenly, shaking me to my core. This traumatic event, coupled with my mother's recent illness, actually accelerated my inner growth. I attended Caroline Myss's workshop in Mexico entitled "The Seven Chakras and the Seven Sacraments," which was a monumental experience. I never stopped crying the whole week. The workshop precipitated a feeling of being reborn—of coming home to my authentic self. This was such a deep spiritual awakening that I turned my life over to God and made a conscious choice to devote my life to service.

Shortly thereafter, Jeff was brought into my life. Within a very short time, I knew that he was my spiritual partner. I immediately felt as if we had always known each other. Jeff professed that he wanted to be together forever. He did not care whether we married or lived together, just as long as we were partners, committed to contribution.

Having been single so long and having worked on healing my past wounds, I had developed a very strong identity as an individual and now was ready to build the "we" necessary for a spiritual partnership. I met Jeff when I was forty-seven and, because I had not married before, I needed to formalize our union by having an actual wedding, not just living together. For the same reason, I also needed to take his last name as my own so we could develop the true partnership I always dreamed of.

The last chapter in this book describes spiritual partnership. Although it's not common, it's something we can all aspire to once we get on the path to psychospiritual healing and growth. In this chapter, written by Jeff and me, we relate the divine story of how we met.

GAIL

I was raised with two sets of parents. My parents and I lived in a two-flat apartment on the second floor, and Aunt Libby, "Unky," and Glenn (my mother's sister, husband and son) lived downstairs. Papa, my maternal grandfather, slept in the family room (which was the basement). The seven of us lived a relatively insular existence. In addition to spending time with the same friends and extended family, we shared most of our meals and all special occasions. In short, we were together all the time.

Both my parents and my aunt and uncle had warm, loving, traditional marriages and gave Glenn and me affection and lots of attention. Though I felt very loved and cared for on one level, I also grew up feeling inadequate and insecure, always viewing Glenn as the "bright one."

While we lived as "one big happy family," the reality was that our home was an emotionally—as well as physically—"boundaryless" environment, where everyone lived and breathed everyone else's business. How I felt and what I thought blurred into what my family thought and felt. As I grew up it became almost impossible for me to make decisions without consulting with the whole clan and getting their approval. At the time, I remember thinking how much luckier I was than my friends because I had two sets of parents to love and take care of me. However, now I realize I came from an enmeshed family system in which my feelings and thoughts were regarded as secondary to those of my family.

When I started dating, I always chose nice guys. Since I had Dad, Unky, and Papa as solid role models, I naturally gravitated toward boys and, later, men with good traditional values—men whom I liked but with whom I never felt a deep inner emotional connection. Though I couldn't have articulated this concept back then, I was always dating and forming attachments purely from my head and not from my heart and soul.

Fearing the disapproval of the clan, I never gave credence to my inner voice that frequently told me to do the exact opposite of what my family suggested. I often had days and sometimes weeks where I experienced feelings of disassociation—as if a part of me left my body and I was observing from a distance what I said and did.

I married at twenty six, which was later than most of my friends, who at that age were already becoming pregnant with their second children. I realized that my marriage did not arise from any significant love; it was simply what was expected of me.

My first husband (my son's father) was a reserved, intelligent, warm man whom my family liked and respected. Throughout the marriage, I felt restless and very disconnected from my husband, rarely able to share my most vulnerable self. I knew my marriage wasn't bad, but at a deep level I was aware it wasn't good either. After nine years of marriage, we parted on good terms. Shortly after my first divorce, I met my second husband. Because I was afraid to be without a man, we married within a few months. On the surface, he appeared more exciting and dynamic than my first. I mistook the excitement and chemistry he generated for love. We divorced just over a year later.

Looking back at both marriages, I see that their demise had nothing to do with the men and everything to do with me. What I had hoped, although not at a conscious level, was that they would fill up that huge, gaping hole of disconnectedness and emptiness that I had felt since I was young.

In reality, the two divorces were blessings in disguise. They forced me to look at how my family dynamics influenced my feelings and behavior. My inner angst drove me into therapy and attending workshops, hoping to learn how to emotionally separate from my family. In coming to grips with my own sense of uniqueness, I finally began to feel like a separate entity, free to make my own decisions in the world.

After my second divorce, I started dating a lot. Men always liked me—mostly because they knew I liked them and had no ax to grind. For many years, I dated, had fun, continued with therapy, read spiritual books, and participated in a myriad of workshops to build my self-esteem.

After years of dating I met Ed, and for the past nineteen years we have been in a committed relationship, although not married. The relationship has satisfied many of my needs even though I've had periods of restlessness. Two years ago my father died (my mother had died many years before), and this traumatic event triggered my need to go inward again, to explore my deepest feelings and emotions. Feeling sad and alone, I retreated into my cocoon, consciously and tenaciously returning to my inner path of self-exploration and discovery.

This shift has me listening to my inner voice as I wrestle with the unsettling aspects of my life: How am I going to actualize my life purpose and be of service to my community? And how is my relationship with Ed going to reflect my inner longing to feel deeply connected to a man at an emotional and spiritual level? I am now living with these questions.

CONVERGING PATHS

We met in 1986 while teaching at the Learning Annex in Chicago. We were both interested in working with singles. As we shared our beliefs and personal histories, we found that our ideas and backgrounds were complementary, yet different. As our personal stories convey, we have both struggled with various issues, valued learning and personal growth, and wanted to share these lessons with others. We became wise as we learned from our mistakes.

Professionally, Gail was an educator who focused on "outside skills," while Basha, being a clinical psychologist, focused on the internal. Gail had been married, was a successful dater, and was in a committed relationship. Basha was single, had never married, had had several soul mate relationships, and was also a successful dater. Therefore, we were the perfect combination to create a program where singles could get support as well as learn the skills to achieve the results they wanted in their dating lives.

After a great deal of work, we put together a six-week program entitled "Taking Charge of Your Single Life." Slowly, over the years as we transformed ourselves, so did the groups. Additionally, our evolution seemed to coincide with the growing spiritual movement. It became clear that most of our clients needed to do psychological and spiritual growth and healing before they could date, let alone mate, successfully.

Personal growth and healing is achieved through the marriage of psychology and spirituality called *psychospiritual* healing. Psychospiritual healing begins when we realize that we are responsible for our lives. The unhealthy thought and behavior patterns that have become part of who we are must be recognized, addressed, and understood. We must look at our childhood wounds and belief systems and acknowledge how they might sabotage our relationships today.

Over time, our work with groups moved from a psychoeducational to a psychospiritual (a thinking to a feeling) focus, and we were amazed with the results. A significant number of our group members found their soul mates. Others talked about how much better they now felt about dating and how we had created a new model for dating and mating that allowed them to date with a sense of purpose, based on their values, beliefs, and interests. Not only did they have the tools to date and mate successfully, but they rejoiced in discovering their inner essence.

This book is the culmination of significant work. As individuals, we've had to confront many issues. As a "couple" together, we've had our struggles. We are definitely soul mates.

Even though we consulted with each other during the writing process, we decided to write this book with two separate tones, reflecting our individual perspectives and expertise on our divergent paths. Basha wrote "Introduction and Philosophy," "The Seven Spiritual Wisdoms," and "Soulwork Steps." Gail was responsible for "Soul Dating Steps" and "The Relationship Continuum." Jeff and Basha wrote the last section, "Spiritual Partnership."

Throughout this book, we emphasize the importance of learning, consciousness, personal responsibility, knowing and loving ourselves, meaningfulness, and presenting ourselves authentically. Throughout the years, we have grown tremendously as individuals and as a team. We promise you that the gifts and potential rewards received during this soul dating process greatly overshadow the times when the path may be difficult and painful. We loved the journey and adventure in writing this book. We hope it will be as meaningful for you reading this book as it was for us writing it.

Welcome to the Wisdoms!

The Seven
Spiritual Wisdoms

The Seven Spiritual Wisdoms present a new way of looking at life and partnership. They are the foundation for leading a life of abundance, fulfillment, and joy, which, in turn, encourages and supports the creation of a sacred union. These Seven Spiritual Wisdoms offer new perspectives that will help you understand the world in ways that facilitate your journey through it, especially as you search for your soul mate or spiritual partner. It is important to understand and use the Seven Spiritual Wisdoms as you travel through the relationship process. In addition, you must live them before, during, and after the dating and mating journey.

The Seven Spiritual Wisdoms

1. Be conscious.
2. Life is meaningful.
3. A human being is a soul and a personality.
4. Value the "being" inside.
5. Love ourselves.
6. Become a whole person.
7. Travel on the path.

Although this type of information is available in various psychological and spiritual books, we are taking this material to a new level of understanding and applying it specifically to relationships.

The art of soul dating and soul mating occurs naturally when you have acquired intimate knowledge of yourself intellectually, emotionally, and spiritually. We invented these Seven Spiritual Wisdoms to help you to consciously discover, honor, and value who you are. It is our goal to support your process with concrete steps to take you along your journey.

We have purposefully chosen the number seven. This number is thought to be the "Way to God" and has been significant throughout history in many ways including: Days of the Week, Colors of the Rainbow, Notes in the Musical Scale, Chakras or Energy Centers of the Body, Sacraments, Levels of Sefirot in the Kaballah, and Wonders of the World. We hope that an understanding of these Seven Spiritual Wisdoms will enable you to embark on a path toward spiritual enlightenment and successfully utilize our philosophy in finding a soulful life partner.

In *The Road Less Traveled*, M. Scott Peck stated that "life is difficult." Most of us resist the wisdom found in this truism. This resistance is especially apparent when we date; we look for "easy" ways to find a partner and we embrace "rules" that promise relationship shortcuts. However, these shortcuts lead to unhealthy outcomes. Rather than accept the inherent difficulty of the dating and mating process and make peace with it, we struggle mightily against and/or refuse to see what is. We are out of step with the rhythm of the truths of life.

When we created and defined these Seven Spiritual Wisdoms, much thought and introspection was put into determining their proper sequence. It is not necessary to take a linear, step-by-step approach because each Wisdom is both independent of and interdependent on the others. We have put them in their current order because we felt that each one builds on the other in a holistic framework.

Please understand as you enter the world of the Seven Spiritual Wisdoms that we believe they reflect the way the world actually is. We have designed them to help you become the person you were meant to be as well as lead you to a divine soul mate or spiritual partnership.

Be Conscious

1

By becoming conscious you accept responsibility for your life. Unconscious human beings usually strive for goals that other people set for them. They accept and embrace others' values and rules because they have not developed their own belief system and identity. They devote their efforts to vain pursuits, only to discover they are wasting time through pursuing illusionary goals and engaging in unnecessary struggles. Conscious people, on the other hand, never lose sight of who they are and feel free to follow their own beliefs.

Take, for example, the endless search for the perfect partner. Most people on this journey embrace the erroneous belief that passion is love. No wonder most relationships don't work out. We try to escape from life with its trials and tribulations and look outside ourselves to others for the secret to eternal happiness.

Becoming conscious is like moving from the darkness into the light. Suddenly, we can see clearly. We consciously concern ourselves with living life fully, seeing and accepting the realities and truths about ourselves and other people, and accepting the laws of the universe. To attain this goal, we must adopt a multisensory perspective when interacting with the world. We must learn to value our intuition and feelings, and not rely on logic in every decision we make.

This new awareness occurs when we rethink our life and its priorities. However, before reinventing ourselves we must take an honest self-inventory and begin to acknowledge our secret (shadow) parts, those we hide from ourselves and from others. We must ask ourselves, "Am I choosing to be the creator of my life, or am I just responding as an observer, a reactor to circumstances?" Becoming conscious involves slowing ourselves down, taking time to "be" so that we can look inward, consistently monitoring our bodily sensations and feelings while embracing the values of truth, love, responsibility, and compassion.

Becoming conscious or embracing a new level of awareness entails living our life knowing that our real work is to know what we think and feel and to be proactive in living our life so that it represents who we are. The questions we need to ponder are: What are our life's dreams? What is our belief system? We must become an observer of ourselves, without judging, and be able to evaluate our behaviors and attitudes. We need to see ourselves through other people's eyes. We can do this only by living a life that values seeing and admitting the truth about ourselves without illusion. Truly understanding ourselves involves a level of knowing which transcends the obvious and helps us actualize our true potential.

We suffer in relationships when we don't see reality clearly. This often manifests as a gender difference. A woman usually falls in love with a man's possibilities, trying to mold him into her idea of perfection. A man, on the other hand, idealizes the woman initially, seeing her as perfect and matching his external ideal. Both, however, are failing to see clearly and value who the other person is, including their strengths and weaknesses. To enter into healthy relationships we must seek reality and not strive to confirm illusion.

In addition to seeing ourselves clearly, then, it is also essential that we observe and clarify who our potential partner really is. This entails consciously observing the other's behavior and asking questions for clarification. We must evaluate their answers to make sure they match our own dreams, goals, and values. This process involves introspection as we learn to rely on our intuition and feelings. Enduring love is possible only when we can let go of our fantasies concerning our partner. When our priority becomes consciousness, soul mating and spiritual partnership are possible.

When we are living as unconscious individuals, we see our interpretation of people and situations as the *only* reality. Therefore, our interpretation of events is totally contingent on where we stand and how we look at things. There is no one reality.

Each of us has a unique perspective, in part influenced by our past life experiences, through which we filter all input. Our interpretation of this data is our reality. Different perspectives give different points of view and reflect corresponding belief and value systems.

We can't separate ourselves from our history, social circumstances, and perspective without doing some "lifework." We can't simply declare ourselves free of prejudices or old learned behavior and instantly replace them. We can become a compassionate observer of our history and perspective without judging ourselves or the circumstances. Only by understanding how our beliefs were formed and influenced can we change them and reinvent ourselves and, in turn, our reality.

The power we assume in taking charge of our lives has to do with our attitude and how we choose to see and evaluate every situation. Cognitive behavioral therapy can be so effective because it is based on altering our thinking to effect change.

One of the hallmarks of a conscious and happy person is being able to see, understand, and value different perspectives. Once you recognize that there are different ways of looking at things, you see that you have many choices. Having these choices puts you in control of your decisions. You are free to choose the most effective action to achieve the results you desire.

Conscious individuals are optimistic realists when interacting with life. They know they can create a peaceful and contented life that supports who they are simply through their mental outlook. They know that on days when they are down and all hope seems to be gone, it's not the world but their mental attitude that needs changing, since *most* of life is out of their control. They are empowered to change from acting helpless to taking charge of their lives. Their lives are transformed each day as they change the way they look at circumstances, utilizing a new perspective or lens. Free will lies in learning to make wise choices in response to events. As they increase their choices, their lives become enriched.

Driving yourself crazy over something you can't change or control is pointless, although very human. It can occur in the most trivial situation or in a deep, meaningful one—for example, someone whom you find attractive does not call (trivial) or someone you love tells you the relationship has to end because he or she is not ready for a commitment (deep). Unconscious people expend energy trying to change a situation they can't control. They suffer as they blame themselves or others and exhaust their energy on things over which they have no control. In other words, if they could simply surrender the impossible dream, they would have the energy to tackle the possible ones.

Once we do everything possible to change the event or learn from it, we can stop putting ourselves through unnecessary pain if we accept the situation for what it is. If a relationship ends we must make peace with what is and find someone who will willingly meet our needs instead of continuing to agonize over the past. Helen Keller wrote, "When one door of happiness closes, another opens; but often we look so long at the closed door that we do not see the one which has been opened up for us." Unconscious people get stuck trying to change reality, which causes significant suffering in dating and relationships. We can increase our power by checking out the values, feelings, and beliefs of others as we interact with them in a relationship.

Accepting reality doesn't mean giving up. It's exactly the opposite. Once we have made peace with the situation, we become more willing to take a risk. Our power is in our attitude. This sounds very simple but is difficult to accomplish due to our need for control. That's why letting go of old belief systems has to be a conscious process, repeated over and over until we can make peace with the situation and move on.

Another principle of being conscious is to accept the laws of the universe. One law is that life changes and is uncertain. But no matter how difficult things seem, we always have choices. Our power is in deciding how we think, feel, and act in every situation. We know there is no external security in life. We must accept that uncertainty is natural and plan for it, even expect it. We always have to consider alternative options. Choice is not ruled by following "shoulds" that are dictated by family, society, or culture. It is simply making a decision that supports us.

A person living in an unconscious way has the conviction that problems are unacceptable and obsesses over them and painfully struggles through life. A conscious person lives with joy, knowing that these struggles lead to eventual solutions. These solutions then present new problems because we are all here to learn lessons.

Living as conscious individuals, we understand that problems and mistakes of the past can never be fully erased. As we become more competent at handling what life throws our way, we just handle problems more quickly and suffer less. We can become proud of our past and learn from our mistakes. We forgive ourselves for unfulfilled promises from the past and consciously choose how we want to live our lives in the present. An individual must live consciously in order to be available for a soul mate relationship. However, spiritual partnership is only possible when both partners embrace the conscious journey in light and travel together, inventing the "we."

Life Is Meaningful

Embracing the Wisdom that life is meaningful is essential in our journey toward a soul mate or spiritual partnership. Somewhere within us lies an intense yearning for a spiritual interpretation of life and a heartfelt connection to the universe. The restlessness and dissatisfaction we often experience arise from our feelings of being disconnected from this universal energy. This emptiness is also caused by a sense of homesickness for our essence, or the soulful qualities that fulfill us. To maintain balance in our lives, our secular lifestyles need to include true values and faith. We must practice service, love, and compassion along with a reverence for our true spiritual nature. This step along the path to spiritual wholeness touches our lives in a profound manner.

Each of us also yearns for a soulful and heartful connection to a life partner. When this level of connection is not present, many individuals feel a deep hunger and longing for more. Soulful relationships are based on the ability to share our heart with another. This connection relies much more on internal bonding than on external values, interests, and beliefs. This can only occur when we have made peace with ourselves and our lives. Emptiness and dissatisfaction describe individuals who have not found purpose and meaning. If our life is meaningful, we are happy and content. That's why embracing meaningfulness in life is so essential to the formation of a soul mate or spiritual partnership.

An authentic spiritual journey allows us to enter a special place where love can flourish. However, we can frequently sabotage ourselves in this realm. Our personality, our "looking good" facade, prevents us from connecting with our divine nature. We need to find truth in our hearts, not be influenced by the opinions of others.

There are numerous pathways to discover our relationship with God or universal energy. We may not need religion but we do need meaning in our lives. We do not have to believe in God or use the word "God" to experience our essence, our soul, and our connection to the universe. It is our thoughts and actions, how we choose to live and experience our lives, that is important, not the words we use. God cannot be known in our mind, so this divine connection must be experienced in our heart.

When you begin the journey toward meaningfulness, you acknowledge that there is a life force that creates everything. The secret to staying connected to this life force is to listen intently with your heart, spirit, and intuition. To establish and maintain this connection, you need to set aside a time and place for this intuitive kind of experience to happen. When you are dealing with spiritual issues or situations, your head helps you process the information but should not be the guide. In other words, your head can only manage, not direct. You need to create the space and open your heart for the divine to enter.

How deeply we embrace and trust the divine is the degree to which we find ourselves in a personal relationship with a higher power. When we come to know our inner God, which is our higher self, we will appreciate that the divine is in everything. This experience is comforting and empowering and makes us feel more alive. This vision of being connected to the divine enhances our sense of how and where we belong, as well as giving us an understanding of what we must be and do to nurture and heal the world as well as ourselves. The more alive we become, the more obvious our personal relationship is with our higher self. Once this experience happens, we will never be the same and the world becomes filled with magic and miracles.

All of life has meaning. Our cosmic consciousness contains a master plan of which we are not aware. Every new experience is a challenge to our faith since, on a soul level, the way to get the results we want is rarely clear and the obstacles are many. We were never promised a life free from fear and struggle. We must have faith that every person and every experience has come into our lives for a purpose based on the lessons we need to learn. Our spiritual challenge is to decipher the lessons in every encounter. We will make fewer mistakes when we listen to our intuition and hearts as they guide us to our true soul mate or spiritual partner.

Everyone and everything is our teacher in one way or another. As a matter of fact, the situations and people that most upset us are often our best teachers. When seen through this lens, our difficulties become blessings. We can't judge the significance of what has really happened until time passes and we can see the entire picture. We need to trust in the paradox that God's time does not necessarily coincide with ours. We can then live in joy and peace as we learn to flow with the mystery of life.

Faith works on every level. We are not alone in tackling problems. We must ask for guidance, open our hearts, and allow wisdom to come in through our highest self. If we accept this guidance in our lives and cooperate with it willingly, even joyfully, we will see that even the greatest apparent disasters can turn out for the best. Faith and trust allow us to walk in the dark or unknown without fear.

As we explore this realm we must recognize that love and fear are on opposite ends of the continuum. Love expands while fear contracts. Fear grows as we pull away from life, failing to embrace life's possibilities. Entering a "love" place involves uncovering our compassion, both giving and receiving love openly as we interact with life. This connection to our heart occurs as we breathe deeply, being present in the moment. We then can touch life and let life touch us.

Coincidences or synchronicities are God's way of speaking to us, but we must pay attention. Opportunities that we need are there when they are supposed to be. For example, we wake up one morning feeling anxious from an unresolved argument the night before. We open a meditation book that's lying on our table and, miraculously, the right passage appears that will help us resolve our internal conflict. The world frequently surprises us. Blessings often come in disguises and we never know whether a situation is ultimately good or bad, no matter how it feels to us at the time.

The story below, taken from *Sadhana, a Way to God* by Anthony de Mello, illustrates this point beautifully.

❧

GOOD LUCK? BAD LUCK? WHO KNOWS?

There is a Chinese story of an old farmer who had an old horse for till-ing the fields. One day the horse escaped into the hills and when all the farmer's neighbors sympathized with the old man over his bad luck, the farmer replied, "Bad luck? Good luck? Who knows?" A week later the horse returned with a herd of wild horses from the hills and this time the neigh-bors congratulated the farmer on his good luck. His reply again was, "Bad luck? Good luck? Who knows?" Then when the farmer's son was attempting to tame one of the wild horses, he fell off its back and broke his leg. Every-one thought this very bad luck. Not the farmer, whose only reaction was, "Bad luck? Good luck? Who knows?" Some weeks later the army marched into the village and conscripted every able-bodied youth they found there. When they saw the farmer's son with his broken leg, they let him off. Now was that good luck? Bad luck? Who knows?

❧

Life is meaningful when we are able to live in the moment. It is an awe-some experience to allow the richness of each moment to speak for itself. Each day is a miracle when we value the journey as much as our destination.

In order for life to be complete, our universal quest for meaning must also be connected to the things we do on a daily basis. We often complain that life seems empty and lacks fulfillment and satisfaction. Yet our time is filled with "doing" activities based on "shoulds" or appearances. Following this lifestyle distracts us from meaningful pursuits that are nurturing to our soul.

Living in the moment allows us to appreciate and feel gratitude for our talents and abilities, acknowledging our gifts. This sense of gratitude also needs to be reflected in our relationship with our partner. This feeling en-courages the partnership to expand and flourish. For example, how wonderful it is to be able to cook a fine meal or walk down the street or see a beautiful sunset. How can we not be touched or moved when we take the time to pay attention to the beauty of God's creatures and the awesomeness of nature? This acknowledgment of life's gifts fills us with awe, peace, and true serenity.

When we provide service—helping the poor, feeding the hungry, being kind to our elderly parents—we are fulfilling part of our higher purpose. Imagining ourselves in others' situations and responding in positive ways allows our lives to be full of meaning and we will feel that universal energy is even more present. The call to service is a yearning from the heart to live and move beyond ourselves. There is no greater reward than to use our talents to make a difference in the world. Often the most fulfilling acts of service are the ones that grow naturally out of our God-given abilities, interests, and skills.

We always get back more than what we give. There is a deep satisfaction inherent in working with others. Serving our fellow man is one of the best ways to diminish the power of fear, helplessness, and hopelessness. Unselfish acts help us appreciate life on a deeper level. Sometimes those we help turn out to be our best healers, identifying important spiritual lessons that we can apply to our own lives. As Gandhi consistently pointed out, "Even as we serve others we are working on ourselves."

Personal meaning and purpose is something all of us must seek in our own way. We must struggle to figure out what feels right. We must listen to our hearts and have the courage to fulfill our dreams. As this occurs, we become enthusiastic, childlike, awake, aware, and authentic in all areas of our lives. This is the wondrous end result of a life that has meaning and purpose.

Pursuing our passion in concert with the universe is the ultimate answer to true meaningfulness. Living passionately, with purpose, and providing soulful service each day, truly puts us on a path toward a soul mate or spiritual partnership. This positive energy dramatically affects how we feel about ourselves and, in turn, helps us attract other like-minded individuals. The feeling of "coming home" to oneself when we have a soulful connection can occur only when each partner has meaningfulness in his or her individual life.

A Human Being Is a
Personality and a Soul

3

In order to lead a fulfilling life and begin the path toward spiritual partnership, we need to understand the components that comprise a human being. We must acknowledge that every person is a combination of soul and personality, reflecting inner and outer qualities. One of the steps to becoming whole is when both components align so that our soul may inspire and direct our personality. Both soul and personality must be active and in alignment when looking for a soul mate or spiritual partnership.

As you read about the distinctions between soul and personality, keep in mind that they are complementary and support each other through life. Both components are needed to be successful. They are also what makes each of us special and unique.

WHAT IS PERSONALITY?

Our personality is the part of ourselves that we use in dealing with day-to-day life. It exists in the material world, manifesting itself mostly through the five senses: taste, touch, smell, seeing, and hearing. The external realms of life are valued. In turn, *what* we do is that which is encouraged and prized by society, our family, and friends. We are defined by *what* we do, not *who* we are. This complete focus on the end result of our activities overshadows and undervalues our internal process. The personality is always chasing after the illusion of perfection.

The personality also values the facade of looking good. It seeks knowing the correct answer, external security, and success. Women pursue success based on superficial values such as beauty and relationships. Men pursue success based on intelligence, power, and money. The personality values competition and, in turn, strives to dominate the physical world to survive—the personality believes in the survival of the fittest.

WHAT IS SOUL?

The soul is that part of our being that transcends the five senses. It is part of a magical realm, not apparent to our everyday eyes. The soul comprises the intuitive and feeling parts of our nature when they are connected beyond our personality to our higher self. The soul experiences our divine nature and energy and allows us to go beyond the explainable levels of our conscious mind. This connection to God and the universe characterizes our spirituality, which is the essence of the soul. The soul lives by the universal law that we are perfect the way we are and we exist to learn lessons and grow. The soul values cooperation and "being." We define "being" as bringing ourselves to the moment with no ulterior motive or goal other than the enjoyment or appreciation of the experience. It is directed by the heart, where life just happens and we flow with events instead of trying to control them.

At birth, we are directly connected to divine or universal energy. We are born with our soul. Our personality's development is influenced by our environment, family, and society and infused with genetics.

Problems arise in our lives as we grow from infancy to school age to adolescence. This is the primary time for the personality to develop. During this time, our driving need to fit in with society's expectations and create an acceptable identity often relegates our soul to the back burner and we lose touch with our true values. Because society's values can be so different from the soul's, we lose understanding and connection with our true essence. How often are we asked who we are and respond by describing what we are or do? We allow the personality to have supremacy over the soul.

As we age, instead of embracing the best parts of both the soul and the personality, we discount one part or the other. We value either the "being" or the "doing" world. Finding an equitable balance between soul and personality is a true goal of an enlightened individual. Realizing that both parts are integral to spiritual growth is one of our most important lessons.

Working toward spiritual partnership has a double reward. It's the perfect opportunity to become more of who we want to be, aligning our soul and personality, and achieving inner fulfillment, with the likelihood of a spiritual partnership developing.

In order to really be and to align with another, we must know and accept ourselves and our partner on many levels. A soul connection occurs when two whole people come together, valuing intimacy and the commitment to learning and growing as well as inventing a life together as partners. This connection is the feeling of "coming home" to ourselves and our partner, a deep level of comfort and acceptance of imperfections, warts and all.

We often don't rediscover our soul until some outside crisis or inner feeling of emptiness occurs. At this point, we begin separating from pure personality issues and begin integrating soul values in our evolution. Generally, this journey fully manifests during adulthood, when we start questioning the meaning and purpose of life.

The alignment of soul and personality is not an easy journey. The existential crisis that prompts this integration is usually an inner calling or an external trauma. Events such as a breakup in a relationship, the death of a family member or friend, an addiction or depression, or the internal feeling of emptiness in our lives focus us on soul or spiritual values. This forces us to reexamine our belief systems, relationships, and lifestyles, to find out what went wrong. In other words, we slowly peel our onion—shed our protective layers and get to our love—to return to our soul or essence. When the energy of the soul is recognized, acknowledged, and valued, it naturally begins to infuse the life of the personality.

This journey of integrating our soul and personality shifts our attention from viewing the world in front of our eyes to viewing it from the inside, through our new consciousness. By doing this, we are further along in the process of meeting our soul mate or spiritual partner.

Value the "Being" Inside

In order to be successful in life, especially in the arenas of soul mating and spiritual partnership, we need to be competent in both "doing" and "being" activities.

Most of us enjoy "doing," and are successful, accomplished "doers." We lead hurried lives where the goal is to accomplish a desired result, look good, or behave the correct way. "Doers" value logic, thinking, financial success, athleticism, a great personality, and physical attraction. The end result is always judged by external standards that society has set for us.

4

"Being" is the exact opposite. It's an attitude toward life where we honor ourselves for being human. "Being" just is, there is no judging. It is the time, when either alone or with others, we focus on honoring our soul by embracing the connection to our higher self, God, and the universe, while acknowledging our spiritual and emotional needs. The "being" state allows us to slow down and live in the moment, to embrace our feelings and intuition, our sixth and seventh senses. It also encourages the expression of our internal values, such as compassion, love, generosity, and kindness, to flourish. These are the ingredients that allow for soul connections.

The essence of the soulful connection is intimacy, unconditional love, shared feelings, listening, and spending quiet time together—all "being" qualities. These are often the exact opposite of values that have encouraged us to be successful in our careers. Therefore, many of us cannot achieve this soulful experience because we have lost the "being" part of ourselves. We have spent most of our lives ignoring or suppressing feelings because we are too busy to address them in our external lives. We don't trust our intuition (our inner voice) and we deny its influence. When we finally have some quiet time, we often ignore our feelings and intuition, fearful that we will be overwhelmed and forced to reassess our lives. We reject them until we become numb, diseased, or depressed and only examine these feelings in crisis.

The minute something arises that makes us fearful or uncomfortable, any kind of pain or negative feeling, we leave the "being" state. Our reaction is to run and "do." Our society values accomplishments and end results, not the internal processing or emotionality inherent in our lives. In a world filled with "doing" there are standards and conditions by which a result is judged. Someone will be better in a particular realm. We often feel unworthy.

We are a society of human "doers" who have lost touch with our real essence. How else could we treat ourselves and others the way we do? Money and success are the bottom line. No wonder so many marriages fail and we have an epidemic of depression and stress, a loss of self. Finding a soul mate or spiritual partner in this condition is impossible.

Fortunately, valuing and embracing the "being" state is a goal that all of us can achieve. All we need to do is to slow ourselves down enough to spend time being introspective, remembering who we are and what is really important and meaningful to us in life. We must remember that every human being is a sacred entity. It is enough to just "be." You don't need to do any specific thing to prove your worthiness to others. Living in "being" is nurturing. It replenishes and helps you prepare for what lies ahead.

"Being" is essential to loving ourselves unconditionally. This self-love is valuing and knowing who we are (soul) as well as what we are (personality). Descartes should have said, "I be, therefore I am." The who is always present and is served by the what. In other words, what you do supports who you are and creates a "being" spirit, aligning the soul and personality in a harmonious relationship. We may apologize for what we did in a particular situation, never for who we are. No one can judge our "being" experience. It can never be taken away; it is one area where we have complete control and is truly a gift to cherish.

The alignment of our soul and personality begins when we start valuing tranquility, feelings, and intuition. Valuing "being" is taking the time to slow down and live in the moment, to hear our inner voice speak. This inner voice reminds us who we really are. We face our fears and limitations in these quiet times. This is the voice of our greatness as well as our humanity. This is the deep knowing that we should take time to experience and accept.

The inner voice is like having our own resident counselor on call. This voice, and that of our higher self, reinforces our awareness that we are not alone and that there indeed is a plan. It encourages us to live in the unknown and embrace the full mystery of life. There is great comfort in considering that we are being looked after and a master plan guides us, if we take the time to listen and embrace it.

We all are capable of listening. The distinction is not whether we can but if we will. Listening implies trust that we will be taken care of. Listening forces us to confront our fears by acknowledging our intuition as we surrender to the messages from our higher self. It's the releasing of our safety net, leaving our old identity and reinventing a new way of "being."

Many of us are frightened to acknowledge this voice when it imposes change. For example, we're scared to end our old patterns of dating or to give up our romantic illusions. We'd rather fantasize about the man or woman of our dreams than start searching for a partner who will emotionally support us.

People who listen and encourage their inner voice through quiet contemplation often say they feel a personal connection with an energy that offers support and reassurance. Whatever we call this voice, be it inspiration or intuition, it is comforting to know that we aren't alone and can summon help and guidance at any time. This acceptance allows our being to flourish and nurtures both our soul and our personality.

We need to make a conscious effort to slow down and engage in "being" activities. This is a frightening endeavor for those of us who lead a hectic "doing" life. Examples of "being" activities are listening to great music, meditating, journaling, walking silently and slowly in a beautiful location, taking a warm bath. Even doing nothing can be a glorious "being" activity, where you can examine inner feelings and contemplate concerns beyond the five senses. The activity does not matter. It is your personal choice that determines what actions will warm and nurture you. Each of us feels wonderful about different experiences. It is solely the participation in these activities that makes us feel satisfied and "filled up." They support the essence of who we are.

Pay attention to how often your inner voice speaks to you. The more attuned you are to your higher self and you take the time to go inward, the more often you will be spoken to and supported from that realm. Optimally, checking in with yourself a couple of times of day will keep you in touch with your inner voice. If you listen and honor what the message says, it will remind you of who you are and bring you back to yourself and what's really important.

As you can see, both human "doing" (personality) as well as human "being" (soul/spirit) are integral to life. "Doing" comes naturally to most of us. "Being" is a more contemplative skill we acquire as we become more conscious. "Doing" is the career work and development of skills to be effective in the world. It deals with changing the universe. "Being" is concerned with the understanding of the universe and helps transform our lives. It is also necessary in order to have a soul connection with another. We must value and honor all our parts to become a complete and loving individual. The integration of both "doing" and "being" is necessary in the development of a soul mate or spiritual partnership. Remember, loving someone is not only a "doing" activity, it's also a "being" experience.

Love Ourselves

Why is loving ourselves so important? This Wisdom contends that our primary relationship is not with a beloved, but with ourselves. Understanding that we cannot love another without first loving ourselves is the foundation of any healthy relationship. This concept of self-love is grounded on the premise that we must accept and love ourselves without conditions. This kind of love expresses a quality of spirit, allowing us to embrace our shortcomings and doubts by acknowledging our individual strengths and weaknesses without judgment. Through this acceptance, we have the strength and security to prepare for a spiritual partnership.

Romance begins when we know and experience our essence. We must find and embrace our soul so that we can share our whole selves with our intimate partner. Desiring a loving partner requires conscious acceptance of all our parts, both positive and negative, being comfortable in our skin. If we have not learned how to be intimate with ourselves, how can we be close to another? Once we embrace all our qualities, we will be able to submit fully to a loving spiritual relationship. Nothing attracts a soul mate more than being someone who opens up completely and is both strong and vulnerable. This acceptance is the beginning of a romance where souls unite.

We all exhibit positive and negative qualities, strengths and weaknesses. Self-esteem is about demonstrating positive regard for ourselves, regardless of our physical and emotional attributes. Whether we're beautiful or plain, brilliant or average, personable or intro-

5

"To communicate is the beginning of understanding. To feel is the beginning of self-growth. To touch is the beginning of involvement. To love ourselves, the beginning of all that will ever be."

—ANONYMOUS

verted, healthy or ill, we need to regard ourselves in a positive light. Our strengths and our weaknesses, along with our gifts and our imperfections, all complete the symphony of who we are—a special human being.

Self-love is being our own best friend through all the difficulties in life, not just when everything is going well. Because we crave the kind of nurturing love we expect a parent to have for a child and many of us never received this as children, we now need to parent ourselves, to be loving, nurturing, and accepting especially during difficult times. As we begin parenting ourselves, we will feel safe and the barriers between ourselves and others will diminish. This is essential for intimacy and friendship, which are the basis of a soul mate relationship.

Most of us come from dysfunctional, critical families. We were judged by some outside standard that parents, society, and friends dictated. Who we were as individuals was not taken into account. Love also came with conditions: "You look wonderful but . . ." and "How come you didn't get an A?" Love was expressed through judgment rather than through compassion and acceptance.

Most of us felt and still feel that we have to earn love and that we are only lovable if we meet certain standards. In response to this, some of us become overachievers, afraid to stop striving for fear we won't be admired or loved. Others stop trying altogether, stating, "Why even try, I won't be successful anyway." If our parents, who loved and wanted the best for us, were judgmental and critical, what can we expect of others? We must learn that a healthy relationship involves accepting, encouraging, and understanding, not judgment and power struggles.

The fifth Spiritual Wisdom reinforces learning and valuing something that most of us were never taught—loving ourselves and, in turn, another, unconditionally. Knowing your partner fully and wanting the best for him or her, and nothing more, is what love is. This is not an easy process. How can someone else love us when we find it difficult to love and like ourselves?

Loving ourselves is forgiving ourselves for being human. It is accepting that humans cannot be perfect. Loving ourselves means striving for excellence on the path of "becoming the best possible me." It is knowing that, within realistic limits, we can accomplish anything.

Embracing the attitude that we are here to grow, learn lessons, and accept our humanity can greatly help us on this journey to find self-love and commitment. This will guide our lives and direct our actions and intentions on a daily basis.

Consider the mistakes we make each day. Many of us feel that we are damaged or unworthy if we can't do or accomplish some specific task. We cannot fully love ourselves because we don't understand what making a mistake actually means. When we make a mistake, we know what to do, we just don't know how to do it. To avoid a mistake, we must simply learn new skills, and most things can be learned. Treat mistakes as a learning experience with the goal being to learn the skills, not to beat yourself up. Making a mistake is not a no-win situation. It is an opportunity to learn appropriate actions to achieve success.

For example, let's suppose you have been attracted to critical men or women who continually reject you. A variety of explanations can be offered for selecting these partners, such as critical parents or childhood rejection. Most of us choose to be victims in this circumstance because we don't know another way to assess the situation. When this happens, we often blame ourselves or another and feel so ashamed that we go into seclusion. When we feel strong enough, we start dating again, but repeat this destructive pattern as, coming from critical parents, this behavior is all we know.

However, there is another way. To change this pattern, we can declare ourselves incapable of doing it any better at this point. We then must become introspective to discover a new approach to handling this problem, or find someone to teach us the appropriate skill. The loving way to look at this breakdown (something negative in life that stops us from our normal routine) is as an opportunity to learn and grow. When we recognize a destructive pattern in our lives we must forgive ourselves, acknowledging we did our best. This is the beginning of compassion and forgiveness.

The essence of preparing for a soul mate relationship is learning how to love and accept yourself fully, warts and all. In turn, this will allow you to fully love your soul partner, since this type of relationship involves a give-and-take, knowing that neither of you will be perfect in all realms. Partnership embraces changing and learning. It values "being" and living in each moment, not obsessing on the end result. This is the dance of life.

Become a Whole Person

6

In order to seek a soul mate or spiritual partner, we must be far enough along on the journey to wholeness. This journey contains many steps; below are some of the most essential ones:

⬦ Knowing and accepting ourselves
⬦ Clarifying our values, beliefs, and goals
⬦ Acknowledging our abilities and accepting our limitations
⬦ Being responsible for ourselves and our behaviors
⬦ Identifying and healing our past wounds
⬦ Utilizing life's lessons to help us grow
⬦ Committing to our personal learning and growth

In essence, a whole person is an adult with a complete identity. We value "being" and self-fulfillment and have no fear of living alone. We are aware of who we are. We consciously direct our lives and are intimate with ourselves. This encompasses our beliefs, values, and behaviors, the parts we like and the ones we dislike. We value responsibility, compassion, balance, and truth. We are able to handle relationships and breakdowns smoothly.

Relationships, like life, have their ups and downs. In a partnership, at different times, each person takes on different roles, each role demanding different skills. Part of becoming whole is to develop these various skills and be able to use them in the relationship. A renewed consciousness prepares us for a soul mate or spiritual partnership.

When we are at our best, being in a soul mate relationship is not a struggle because we honor intimacy and communication with our partner. We don't belittle or criticize our partner regardless of the circumstances. We support each other's decisions and place ourselves in situations where we can facilitate mutual learning and growth. We are able to recognize our partner's past wounds and use this knowledge to support each other in continuing the healing process. In this way, true partnership can flourish. In essence, until we are far enough along on our journey to wholeness, a "me" in progress should not look for a "we"!

Power struggles are usually present in relationships where each person is not whole. With these struggles, we ask our partner to give up his or her identity or we give up our own; such behavior stems from our individual desires, fears of independence, misplaced projections, or power needs. In the relationship it may appear as if both people have separate lives or that one has given up his or her identity, becoming what the other wants. This relationship pattern usually leads to depression, passive-aggressive behavior, apathy, or anger. The self becomes lost. For either partner, there is no intimacy, friendship, or partnership.

A spiritual partnership requires and a soul mate relationship aspires to two separate "I's" that work together to invent the "we." Each partner does not depend on the other for a sense of self; rather, they complement and further complete each other. As partners, they work on their individual lives and motivate the other to do the same.

In a healthy partnership, we each recognize our individual needs and acknowledge our personal conflicts and emotional baggage from the past. Our reaction to a problem or situation is usually dependent on our perspective, formed mostly from our personal history (what we were taught overtly or covertly by our family and society). Truth is subjective because we each use different filters to assess what is actually happening. There is no one right way to *view* the world, there are only different perspectives. Healthy relationships recognize and actually applaud differences. Together, partners are able to honor and learn from each other's strengths and points of view. When we become more complete we can come to decisions that benefit each of us as individuals, as well as the partnership.

The journey toward wholeness is a work in progress and ultimately provides us with a new perspective. No matter what changes occur on our outside, we are transformed—we feel strong, stable, complete, and able to handle whatever life presents.

Personal growth and healing is achieved through the marriage of psychology and spirituality—psychospiritual healing. Such healing comes from action, not lethargy. Setting boundaries, taking risks, understanding and pushing through fears, being responsible, and making choices are examples of healing actions. Self-love, forgiveness toward self and others, and psychospiritual healing are critical to becoming whole.

Psychospiritual healing commences when we realize that we are responsible for our lives. The unhealthy thought and behavior patterns that have become part of who we are must be recognized, addressed, and understood. We must look at our childhood wounds and belief systems and acknowledge how they might sabotage our relationships today. Examining the past isn't for the purpose of spending the rest of our days agonizing over our unhappy childhood—we can responsibly use these negative experiences as opportunities for change and forgiveness and for learning new skills.

Healing, so that we feel strong and centered within ourselves, involves examining areas of pain and fear. This process is necessary to fully embrace life and to flow with the ups and downs of a healthy relationship. To love deeply, we need tremendous courage and strength. We must face our lives directly, not run from our pains and limitations. We must move toward our fear, accept the fact that we fear, live with it, and face it down. We might unintentionally limit ourselves in our lives and relationships due to a need for security and control, finding that the more choices we have, the more scared we become. Maintaining the status quo might seem safe, yet true security comes only from taking a risk, opening up, and discovering who we really are.

Establishing the body-mind connection necessitates that we be in touch with our feelings, needs, desires, and values. This includes living in our body fully and opening our heart, mind, and spirit to the process of healing ourselves. Most of us have lost touch with these connections. Therefore, we don't know what we really desire.

Intrinsic to our emotional healing is our connection to the heart. We must honor our true feelings and accept them as an integral part of who we are. This links our intellect with our true self. The ability to express our feelings candidly and openly is essential to intimacy. To communicate effectively, we must understand the difference between talking about feelings and feeling our feelings. For most of us, it is easier to run from emotions than to feel. However, unexpressed feelings catch up with us and act in destructive ways. Healthy awareness of problems and communicating well are essential to maintaining a soul mate or spiritual partnership.

Being a whole person also infers that we strive to live a balanced yet full life—one that values both "being" and "doing" activities. Maintaining balance in our lives means spending an adequate amount of time on our bodies, work, play, relaxation, communication, intimacy, family, friends, financial security, contribution, and meaningfulness in life. We are not ready for a healthy relationship unless our life is in balance. This balance keeps us from becoming too needy or losing ourselves in a relationship.

Having self-confidence or self-esteem is also part of becoming whole. It means accepting the real conditions of the world, knowing and being at peace with the idea that people have limits. We cannot do everything and be competent in all areas of life. Self-confidence requires that we accept the world as a place where there are some things we can do and some things we can't, some things we must do, some things we must learn to do, and some things we must ask others to do, all without judgment. We must recognize, accept, and cope with our competencies and failings as well as those of others.

Being whole and complete is also maintaining our dignity by living authentically according to the values that we espouse. In other words, we walk the talk. Instead of needing to be right, we live cooperatively, creating win-win situations with our partner.

Healing our personality, heart, and mind is the psychospiritual work we all must do. When we experience true feelings and emerge from this process as a whole person we can align our soul and personality. As Carl Jung said, "When you find the self you find love." Spiritual partnership does not occur with possession or control but through our capacity to be open, loving, and free.

Travel on the Path

7

As human beings, we're all on a psychospiritual path, searching for wholeness, meaning, and fulfillment. Eliminating the obstacles that prevent us from connecting to our true essence is paramount in this process. Usually the search begins after some kind of emotional catastrophe occurs in our lives and we realize that our external life is empty and meaningless. This emptiness forces us to acknowledge that what was comforting, nurturing, and fulfilling no longer works to satisfy our needs. These surprising and alarming internal changes present an urgent call for change and transformation. This calling begins the search for wisdom and enduring personal values.

Being on the path demonstrates the conscious choice to reunite with your soul. It doesn't matter where you are on this path, only that you are consciously engaged with your wisdom, heart, and intuition. Because you are always in the process of becoming whole and constantly evolving, there is no beginning or end to the path, it's just a road to travel. Being on the path directs us to discover who we really are, to find the fulfillment, purpose, and sense of meaning that is missing in our lives. It is a journey that integrates the spiritual elements with the worldly. It is the beginning of an ongoing commitment to look inward for answers. The path is joyous and full, involving much struggle and effort as well as discipline, courage, and perseverance. The spiritual journey entails falling on our faces, getting up, brushing ourselves off, turning to God or universal consciousness, and taking another step.

This process leads to a life filled with heightened states of consciousness, awareness, wholeness, joy, creativity, and love because our lives are now directed by meaning and purpose. We can replace "I am!" with "Who can I be?" Life becomes a joyful opportunity to grow, love, and contribute to another with an open heart.

The ability to love ourselves is necessary for experiencing the divine in another. Connecting our heart with our mind is a deeply spiritual endeavor that encompasses both blessings and responsibilities. Aligning our soul with our personality is the next level of learning and growing. We must first travel our own path, confronting life and becoming our most authentic self. Only then will we be ready to make a real commitment. Falling deeply in love with ourselves is the only way to learn about unconditional love.

Being on the path means taking the steps that will help us learn the lessons that we need in this lifetime. Many of us react to situations in ways that are directed solely by our personalities. Therefore, we are not consciously making choices. We simply follow what we've been programmed to do, such as:

◇ Not valuing introspection, learning, and growing
◇ Never questioning life's meaning or purpose
◇ Devoting our lives to the satisfaction of our personal needs
◇ Seeking enjoyment through the senses, emotional pleasures, material security, and/or achievement of personal ambition
◇ Living as human "doers"
◇ Valuing the materialistic or physical plane
◇ Not considering contribution or service to others

We are spiritually asleep. Our initial response to adversity is to deny or resist the need to change. As unconscious people, we stuff down our feelings and thoughts with some type of addiction, such as workaholism, codependency, or alcoholism, or we chase our tails because we fear changing our lives and, thus, surrendering to the process of transforming ourselves. Beginning on a spiritual path means ignoring superficial concerns and diving into the deeper waters to discover our soul and our purpose in life. The question we should ask ourselves is, Why do some of us embrace this path sooner, while others keep resisting?

In our lives, we are presented with lessons to learn and problems to solve. We can't escape this subtle call. If we don't listen we will be hit over the head until we do. For example, while dating, you will consistently have dates who are just like your parents. Whatever healing you need to do, your dates will represent those unresolved wounds. Issues such as alcoholism, physical or emotional abuse, or simply dominant or passive behavior will be presented until you resolve them. The negative patterns and unhappiness in your life will continue until you pause, go inward, and become conscious. Once you deal with these issues and begin the healing process, you will find yourself on the path to becoming whole.

Being on this path is a holistic process, not a linear one. There is no cause or effect. Each day is an adventure with no instructions. When we are on the path, we need to learn to live moment to moment and not search for answers. The answers will show up for us in the appropriate time. Then we embrace life as a participant rather than an observer. We each have our own unique journey of soulwork, our own timetable for self-discovery. This is how we need to develop in order to manifest our deepest purpose and potential.

We do not automatically receive wisdom. We only discover it after we journey alone into the unknown territory of our higher selves. The urge to find deeper meaning in life unfolds in a sequence of three steps that exert a slow transformation on us: the Awakening, the Dark Night of the Soul, and the Rebirth.

THE AWAKENING

The Awakening is a time when we, as individuals leading ordinary lives, suddenly find our world disrupted by the spiritual call manifested by a feeling of separation from something deep in our heart and soul. The soul is calling us back home to search for truth, personal authenticity, and meaning. When we respond to the Awakening, we make a vow to our higher self. We are driven by something greater than ourselves—a search for meaning and answers to the existential questions Who am I? and Why am I? This search begins within, where the key to harmony and happiness lies.

Once we start on the path there is no turning back. Once the vow is taken, something greater than ourselves (universal energy or higher purpose) takes over and leads us as we surrender to the process.

The Awakening begins for each of us differently. It can happen suddenly or over a period of time. It is important to keep it alive after it has occurred and to continue on the path. Committing to the path takes great courage and faith because we initially feel so alone on this journey.

THE DARK NIGHT OF THE SOUL

The next part of the journey is a scary, painful, and lonely leap into unknown territory. We don't know what we will discover, which is why this part of the path is called the Dark Night of the Soul. Part of the purpose of this experience is to unveil what we are attached to in our external world that keeps us from trusting in ourselves and our higher consciousness. Dr. Caroline Myss, in *Anatomy of the Spirit*, names this process "calling back your spirit." She emphasizes that after you discover what you are attached to that is taking away your power, you detach and reconnect with this internal power source.

The journey toward wholeness requires that we look honestly, openly, and with courage into ourselves, into the dynamics that lie behind how we feel, perceive, value, and act. It is a journey through our defenses, consciously experiencing the nature of our personality and working to align it with our soul.

We must see clearly our repeated behaviors and outdated belief systems that keep us from being true to ourselves. Rebellion is a natural part of this process. It is healthy and human to question our beliefs. After such times of testing, we return to life authentically. Each belief system and value that we espouse is something we have wrestled with, challenged, and earned, not just something we've been given or had forced upon us.

Whenever we are involved in the process of personal renewal, we must face our shadow and come to terms with it. The parts of ourselves that we wish to avoid or neglect turn out to be the material necessary for real growth. When we embrace all these parts, they slowly become our strength as we turn darkness into light.

It is essential to trust and surrender to this universal or divine process. Profound self-acceptance and wholeness is a search for truth within the darkness. The task of becoming free is to slowly shed these layers to uncover the core truths that transform this experience into healing and self-renewal. This spiritual and psychological journey is a living process that keeps evolving and changing. The Buddhist masters affirm that we evolve through suffering until we learn to evolve through joy.

Initially, the most difficult part of the Dark Night of the Soul, besides the pain, is the feeling that life is beginning all over again and feeling like a stranger inside. As difficult as this experience might be, it is necessary in order to move forward in life. During this process we are forced to live totally in the present moment, disregarding our entire life history as well as any short-term future plans. As uncomfortable as this letting go of our past and future feels, this void allows divine energy to permeate every part of us. We realize that we are never alone on this journey and that universal guidance and wisdom are present, embracing us as we discover our true essence. Getting support from resources like twelve-step programs, a therapist or spiritual counselor who has gone through his or her own inner journey, books, and workshops can also be helpful during this process. (See the selected bibliography.) While you are working through the Dark Night of the Soul, take one step at a time, nurture yourself, and participate in safe and loving relationships that contribute to your individual healing process.

THE REBIRTH

The Rebirth is the process of returning home to the center of our being, returning to the light. After all our hard work, we finally realize that what we have been seeking, we already have. We come home to ourselves. We are radiantly aware of life and live with the joyful freedom of "being."

～

What had been chaotic became simple
What had been confusing became clear
What had been sadly ordinary became sacred and extraordinary.

—*Anonymous*

Individuals who have been through the process of the Rebirth live the following seven tenets:

◇ We are committed to looking at the world without any delusions or distortions.

◇ We are able to examine our attitudes and thoughts and be totally straightforward and honest with ourselves and others.

◇ We are committed to living as we speak and believe.

◇ We are able to stay in touch with who we are.

◇ We are grateful for the opportunity to lead a spiritual life.

◇ Every day we praise and celebrate life's mysteries.

◇ We are grateful for the chance to give back to others what we discovered for ourselves on the path.

Readiness for a spiritual partner comes from life experiences, having made the journey of discovery to what is really meaningful and central to who we are. Once we can accept and honor our dreams, we can allow another person the freedom to follow his or her destiny. We can accept and embrace whatever issues our partner is facing. We have developed the ability to appreciate and value other perspectives.

When you understand how life is, you can accept the mystery of relationships more readily, acknowledging that change is inevitable. And finally, only when you can recognize your soul and live by its values, can you be truly intimate with another.

You now are armed with Seven Spiritual Wisdoms that will prepare you for a soul mate or spiritual partner. Once your potential partner has done his or her work, the universe will bring you together in its mysterious and miraculous way.

Soulwork Steps

The seven steps of soulwork represent the many inter- and intrapersonal issues we need to confront, explore, and heal to fully embrace and utilize the Seven Spiritual Wisdoms. These steps help us begin the inner preparation needed to enter into a soulful relationship and travel on the path toward spiritual partnership.

The following seven steps have been chosen for several reasons. First, all the Seven Spiritual Wisdoms are represented in them, and second, our past experience with clients has shown us that these are critical areas in the healing journey as a prerequisite to begin the soul dating process.

The Seven Steps of Soulwork

1. Move from the darkness into the light
2. Discover the gift of solitude
3. Learn the healing power of forgiveness
4. Embrace the shadow
5. Feel, heal, and move on
6. Attain a balanced life
7. Become the best possible you

We are each on our own path to inner healing, meaningfulness, and wholeness. Our inner preparation for a soul mate relationship, therefore, needs to be individualized, in a step-by-step manner, to fully actualize our potential for a soulful partnership. We each need to determine the level of awareness we must acquire to achieve this goal. Engaging in the following activities helps us reinvent who we are and guides us to become the person we were meant to be.

Remember, we are never alone. Guidance is always available, both spiritual and practical. If we listen and proceed in a heartfelt manner, we will be guided by our higher self to do what is right for us in the moment.

When you explore the Seven Spiritual Wisdoms, you become aware of the particular issues you need to address. For example, after contemplating the Spiritual Wisdom "Life Is Meaningful," one of our clients created the following list of possible items to work on based solely on that Wisdom:

⬧ Seeing the universe as purposeful
⬧ Developing a relationship with a higher consciousness
⬧ Learning and growing from life's experiences
⬧ Living in the moment
⬧ Providing service from the heart
⬧ Finding our own personal purpose in life

As you read the soulwork steps, it will become apparent to you that there is no inherent sequence in this journey; thus, there are several ways you can choose to proceed:

⬧ Begin with the step that seems easiest, to get quick, positive results.

⬧ Choose the step that seems hardest, getting the most difficult out of the way first.

⬧ Choose the step that seems to be the biggest obstacle, keeping you from where you want to go next.

⬧ Trust your heart and begin with the step that seems to resonate with you.

Do take advantage of as much support as possible during this process. Speak with family and friends, refer to books, tapes, and videos, but most of all, be open to the process of self-discovery. We have provided you with a bibliography and list of audiotapes at the end of the book (beginning on pg. 214), but you can also go to the bookstore or library or internet and explore. You'll know the right resource for you because you will be drawn to it.

If you need more direct personal support, depending on where you are on this journey, there are many other resources available, such as twelve-step or self-help groups, individual or group therapy, spiritual and religious counselors, and a variety of workshops.

We suggest that you find a therapist who treats the whole person, one who utilizes a holistic approach to health and wellness. In addition to symptom relief, a fundamental goal of therapy is to generate lifestyle changes by encouraging an integration of emotional (feelings), mental (the cognitive process), spiritual (examining meaningfulness and one's place in the universe), and physical (biochemical and behavior) aspects of the human condition. A holistic therapist believes that the practitioner and client are partners who work together. Both conventional and alternative therapies are utilized to achieve effective results. If you need assistance, contact the American Holistic Health Association (AHHA), an organization that can offer you guidelines as well as referral sources (phone: 714-779-6152; e-mail: ahha@healthy.net).

Please remember, this is a growth process. You must allow time for introspection and appreciation of the changes that are occurring within you. Internalizing the Seven Spiritual Wisdoms and taking guidance from this soulwork should be gradual. Allow yourself time to grow and assimilate the new material into your essence. Remember, it takes at least ninety days to learn and internalize a new behavior.

A word of caution: There is no one answer. Make sure you don't lose yourself in this process. Every source of information helps on your path to becoming who you want to be. Information helps you in different ways and at different times by offering different perspectives. Nor should you get caught up in the language or terminology that we, or anyone else, uses. The most important thing is your ability to utilize and apply the information in a way that continues to support the discovery of who you are. There is no right place to start. Just begin and you'll be guided by your higher self and the universe. Trust the process.

Soulwork Step 1:
Move from the Darkness
into the Light

❧

8

Our deepest fear is not that we are inadequate.
Our deepest fear is that we are powerful beyond measure.
It is our light, not our darkness, that most frightens us.
We ask ourselves, "Who am I to be brilliant, gorgeous, talented and
fabulous?"
Actually, who are you not to be?
You are a child of God, your playing small doesn't serve the world.
There's nothing enlightened about shrinking so that other people
won't feel insecure around you.
We are born to make manifest the glory of God that is within us.
It's not just in some of us; it's in everyone.
And as we let our light shine, we unconsciously give other people
permission to do the same.
As we are liberated from our own fear,
Our presence automatically liberates others.

—NELSON MANDELA, 1994 INAUGURAL ADDRESS

❧

Nelson Mandela's remarkable speech reveals the simple truth that most of us are afraid of living in the light because this demands that we acknowledge our authentic self and, in turn, our magnificence. This is the process of becoming conscious.

A person who is conscious is committed to living in the light. Conscious people are aware that there are choices, and they rationally sort through them before making a decision. Conscious people have fears, but their fears don't prevent them from living life fully. They value truth and personal responsibility. They embrace change and growth. They continuously check in with their feelings, monitor their fears, and have no illusions about themselves. They know and accept both their own and others' strengths and shortcomings, with no judgment. They see themselves as others see them. They know that their level of self-awareness makes their personal problems more transparent, thus easier to work through.

When we can see life clearly and consciously, we lose our encumbrances and become able to make the right decisions. Living successfully—acknowledging who we really are and being willing to take chances—is critical to this process. Being open to the light, we can begin the process of self-actualization. Being an authentic person by living in the light, accepting our magnificence, and acting courageously is the path we must all embrace in the search for a soul mate or spiritual partner.

Most of us, however, have chosen to interact with life either by running away from ourselves or by becoming a spectator. We perceive it as much safer to live in darkness, never questioning our roles or beliefs or "rocking the boat." Furthermore, living this way, we don't place any expectations on ourselves, and other people don't expect much from us either. In this vein, we focus on striving for safety, sameness, and external security.

Although most of us have chosen to lead our lives in this manner, does it really represent who we want to be? Does this apparently safe place really protect us? And, if so, at what cost to our inspiration and spirit? Why are most of us afraid to live authentically?

As we've been discussing, one reason we fear living in the light is that we would have to be responsible for all our decisions, and that's scary. Another very compelling reason is that it would greatly change the safe and secure interpersonal dynamics within our family and community.

As Dr. Caroline Myss discusses in her book *Anatomy of the Spirit,* we are born into a tribal consciousness or group power. Our "tribe," or family-of-origin, has a certain set of belief systems and behaviors in which every member has a prescribed role. The group's thought form comes first, not the individual's. In this dynamic, the focus is on loving others before ourselves, and we are called selfish when we take care of our own needs first.

The family or tribe feels entitled to tell you how to feel, think, and act in every situation. The expectation of loyalty from the group holds enormous power over you as an individual. They love you, but with conditions.

They don't want you to change. They believe that you must deny your needs in order to please the family or tribe since the group is more important than individual growth and needs. The tribe will do anything to keep you from moving forward, thinking on your own, and claiming your own power, because that will mean change and the likelihood of your separation from the group.

If you don't obey the leaders, they feel betrayed and will punish you to shut down your individuality. This castigation can take on various forms of emotional coercion. They chastise you by becoming cold and critical, or if that doesn't work, they stop talking to you. Some tribes will resort to physical abuse in order to intimidate or control. Each tribe feels justified in using its particular form of duress to get what its leaders believe the group needs. According to group consciousness, it is contrary to the tribe's best interests to value the individual or to allow any belief that the tribe recognizes as a threat.

If you're not internally strong, you'll probably cave in to your tribe's pressure. Gail's story illustrates the power that her family exerted:

In high school, I fell in love with Al. We really had a soulful connection. We were the best of friends and really enjoyed spending time together. My father criticized Al for being "too Jewish." Soon after, I rejected him and we split up. Even today, I still miss what I could have had with him. I sadly realize that I chose the approval of my father over a nurturing and loving relationship because I didn't have a strong sense of myself and therefore could not fight against my father's opinion.

If we do not know and like ourselves, we will easily give over to someone else our power to make decisions in our life. That's living in darkness!

The safety of the tribe is seductive because, in exchange for this obedience and loyalty, we are given many benefits—acceptance in the group, emotional safety, security, and bonding. To be part of a group that tends to many of our needs makes us feel safe and powerful. Support and loyalty give us a strong sense of security and connection to the physical world.

The tribe also tries to convince us that we cannot survive on our own and therefore we can't be responsible for our own lives. To keep us in their web, the members nurture us, mostly when we are wounded. In other words, they value what Caroline Myss calls our "woundology" or the victim mentality.

Basha's story shows how her mother and "tribe" unconsciously sabotaged her individuality:

My mother was always there for me. Whenever I had a problem she would listen and empathize. If my mother was not around, my friends were there to comfort me. I would receive tremendous nurturing while talking about my problems, even though the focus was never on resolution. As good as this felt, the negative side was that I could never manage life on my own. At twenty-seven years of age, I was terrified to go away to graduate school. No wonder I never got married, even though I dated a great deal. I knew intuitively that I needed to know who I was before becoming part of a couple or I would have become lost. I needed to learn to be self-reliant, so I forced myself to move far away from home. How could I become a psychologist or ever get married if I couldn't live and deal with my own problems?

I realize now that I could never have discovered who I was, living at home. I finally understood, in the process of living alone, far away from home, that my mother really needed me more than I needed her. What I also discovered was that by giving in to my "tribe," I was really crushing my self-esteem, remaining in the dark within the security of the system.

At the same time we feel safe and secure inside the tribe, we also have a strong urge stirring inside us to become our own person. We need to live our lives directed by individual power and personal responsibility in the choices we make. When tribal beliefs obstruct our psychospiritual growth, internally we feel a great sense of dissatisfaction and uneasiness, which signals our need to separate. Separation is a difficult process because it requires a psychological, emotional, and physical distance from people we have become bonded to and dependent upon for our very security.

Either we can stagnate by siding with the secure old beliefs (external security), or we must change and separate from familiar people and places that no longer serve us. Becoming conscious is a very courageous and painful process. We need to break free of values that no longer support us.

One of our greatest challenges is being stuck in two places: the old world we need to release and the new one we are afraid to enter because it requires us to become responsible for our lives, without the external security. We know intuitively that once we start owning our power, in even one area of our lives, we can never again use our history as an excuse. We become responsible. We invest energy in the power of our individual spirit by moving into the light and continually coming back to what supports us as individuals. If our spirit is strong enough to withdraw from the power of a group belief, it is strong enough to change our life.

This is the process of individuation and self-growth. We are focused on making decisions and directing our own life. We need to listen internally to what we need. As long as we use comfort and security as our criteria for success, we will fear our own intuitive guidance because, by its very nature, it directs us into new cycles of learning that we are frequently uncomfortable with.

We come alive inside by becoming internally empowered. We have to cross our bridges alone, accepting our own self-love, if we want to transcend to spiritual partnership. To move into the light, we must internalize this vow:

I will always own my power as a priority wherever I am and whoever I'm with. I need to become a complete "I" in order to invent the "we" with my beloved.

SOULWORK

The following questions will help you clarify your journey out of the darkness into living with consciousness. We suggest keeping a journal to contain your responses. As you progress on your own path to self-discovery you can look back at your answers and see your growth. Remember, be as honest as possible; there is no right answer and no one will see your responses except you.

1. Why are you afraid of change? What beliefs do you hold regarding external security and safety? What benefits do you get from living your life by playing it safe? What do you lose from this perspective?

2. What really scares you more, success or failure? What fears do you have that keep you from showing your magnificence to yourself or others? Make a list of your fears and describe how some of them prevent you from growing.

3. What belief patterns (such as "men are not to be trusted" or "don't let anyone see your unlovable parts") did you inherit from your family? Which of these patterns that still influence your thinking—especially in

the area of the opposite sex and dating—can you now see no longer serve your best interest?

4. Focus on finding the light surrounding any situation. You can do this by living in the moment and paying attention. This attention or serenity of the mind is the beginning of contemplation. Each day, practice this new skill by choosing one activity, like eating or walking, and focus on it fully—do only that activity for fifteen to twenty minutes. Be fully present in the experience without evaluating it. Remember, be mindful of what you are doing. Consider all the times you have eaten a meal mindlessly and, after finishing, you've realized that you didn't even taste the food. Does this sound familiar? Evaluate your daily experience with this new mindfulness. This is the beginning of discovering your magnificence.

5. To live in the light means bringing the unconscious into consciousness. It also means letting go of our fixed habits of perception. In other words, we expect things to look and behave a certain way because they've always looked and behaved that way in the past. If you expect answers to come in a certain pattern or look a certain way, then it will be difficult for new and more expansive answers to arise. Just trust the process. Once you have asked a question, it's important to let go.

Every day, devote some time to "living in the question." Ask a question and be open to the answers. For example, ask yourself, "Why am I having such a hard time finding someone nice to go out with?" or "Why do I avoid spending time participating in 'being' activities?" Listen carefully, because immediately answers will come to you. Write down these answers, without judging them. Be spontaneous. Brainstorm. Consider your fears as they surface. Don't let them stop you.

MEDITATION

I am committed to moving from living in darkness to living in light. I will not let my fears stop me. I know that the more I celebrate my magnificence, the closer I am to connecting with my spiritual partner.

Soulwork Step 2:
Discover the Gift
of Solitude

The last time we saw Rhonda, an attractive twenty-seven-year-old nail technician, she was absolutely glowing. We asked her, "Are you in love?" This was her reply:

9

Yes, I'm in love with me! After dating idiot after idiot, where I felt bruised and abused, I decided to take a break and just spend time alone, sometimes seeing some close friends. At first it was difficult. I had never spent time alone before. I was used to going from one relationship to another.

It's been about six months now and I finally feel like I found myself. I'm much more secure. I like and love me for the first time in my life. I now have the time to reflect on who I am.

I am able to observe other people and see how my friends deal with their relationships. They're how I used to be—needy, insecure, unhappy, suffering, and complaining. I simply lost myself in my relationships.

I laugh now when my friends say to me, "You have to find a boyfriend." I'm actually the only one who is happy and at peace. I've had enough crappy relationships. I know what that's about. Why would I want another?

Now, I don't even know what I saw in my last relationship. I guess I was in it out of fear of being alone. I had to be with someone. My judgment was so out of whack from being so needy. I felt lonely being with him. Now I'm alone and I never feel lonely or needy.

I reclaimed myself. I'm taking the time to know who I am and discover what I want in life, as well as from a relationship with a man. I finally achieved some mental and emotional stability. I know the difference between needing and wanting a man. My values concerning what I'm looking for in a man have changed. I deserve more than just having a man who is fun and is there only in the good times. I give and he takes is no longer acceptable. I never thought I'd say this, but I'd much rather spend an evening reading a book than go on a date if I'm not really interested. I thought I was leading my own life, but I didn't have a clue until I started living alone.

When I'm ready to maintain my own life and enter into a relationship, I'll starting dating again. I want to make sure that I will never get into those destructive kinds of relationships again out of desperation. Now that I've taken the time and discovered that I love my life, I'm not going to give it up. Solitude was the greatest gift I ever gave myself. How else could I have fallen in love with me?

We feel lonely when we become isolated from ourselves, not from others. The gift of solitude is the ability to be totally alone without feeling lonely. Enjoying solitude is a wondrous feeling, directed by our soul as we connect with our higher self and universal energy. In solitude we can separate ourselves from the pressures of the external world, with its expectations and chaos. We can awaken our personal visions, encompassing issues from our past, present, and future. We experience the joy of living in the moment. It is a time to contemplate every facet of our existence and fully appreciate the richness inside ourselves.

Taking time out from normal routines and creating a safe haven for ourselves is not a luxury. It's essential! It's as critical to our healthy existence as our normal daily activities of eating, sleeping, and working. In fact, it's the only experience that fully replenishes us because we are in charge. If we take the time to listen, the sounds we hear in silence are those of our higher self, the quiet and majestic voice of our soul, and we will be guided by divine energy. We can then trust that the unfolding of our lives will present us with valuable lessons.

Solitude can be enhanced by spending some time in nature where we can center ourselves and connect with the universe. There, our inner voice is free to speak, supported by an external quietude and serenity. In essence, we are healed by the universe.

In addition to promoting independence, resourcefulness, and self-love, solitude serves several other important functions:

◇ Maintains boundaries—Until we have a strong sense of who we are and learn to love ourselves, we will be unable to set and maintain healthy boundaries. An example is the ability to say and accept no.

◇ Encourages creativity—Creativity puts us on a path of self-discovery deep inside ourselves. It contributes to our sense of feeling alive and playful. It encourages our search to find innovative ways of dealing with our problems and of serving others.

◇ Replenishes positive energy—Solitude encourages the release of stress through introspection and the replenishment of positive energy. We are able to heal and grieve past losses and change. We are able to reinvent and redirect a new lifepath for ourselves.

◇ Nurtures and renews the soul—This assures our personality and soul will continue their alignment.

We fool ourselves with the illusion that other people are going to make us happy. In truth, we need to make ourselves happy by tapping into our inner spirit and energy. Like Rhonda, instead of expending energy outside ourselves, we need to keep some of this energy. We do this by learning to find the "lover" inside us, which helps ground us and enables us to make a soul connection with another. The goal is to love with desire, rather than need. To do this, we must first be comfortable with who we are, enjoy our own company, and feel that our life is fulfilled.

When we finally emerge from our alone time, we will be able to be fully present with another because we are finally whole and complete within ourselves. We will be able to experience a sense of calm, quiet, and confidence in our true nature. We will glow with the incandescent light of our soul as it is reunited with our personality. Now we will be ready to make our soul connection.

SOULWORK

As you answer the following questions, know that you are taking time for yourself. Do them in solitude—unplug the phone, turn off the TV. Give yourself the gift of time with yourself.

1. What does being in a relationship provide that you can't give to yourself? Does Rhonda's story clarify this? What is the value of solitude for you? Identify the fears and excuses that prevent you from experiencing this solitude. Make a list. Ask yourself: Does each of these excuses and fears really support you or did you inherit this belief from your family or society?

2. Introspection can be one of the easiest activities to postpone, even though it should be one of our most important concerns. Solitude encourages and enhances introspection. The complicated and pressurized world we live in encourages us to immerse ourselves in external patterns without time for self-reflection and direction. In order to start on the path toward soul mate or spiritual partnership, the following questions need to be both thought about in your mind and experienced in your heart and soul during your time of solitude. As you answer them, focus on what supports you, not on what others expect of you:

◇ In what ways are your personality and soul not yet aligned? Why?

◇ What kind of life, and partner, will support the alignment of your soul and personality?

◇ What are the major milestones you are most proud of?

◇ What are your dreams for your life?

◇ Make a list of your priorities. Do these activities presently support your dreams and goals? If not, how can you change them?

MEDITATION

I value the gift of solitude. I know that my time alone will be an opportunity to fall in love with myself as well as hasten the divine connection with my soul mate.

Soulwork Step 3:
Learn the Healing Power
of Forgiveness

10

The ability to forgive both ourselves and others is one of the most important components in healing from past wounds. Forgiveness provides us the opportunity to heal from wounds we don't deserve and allows us to love and be at peace with our personal history, instead of leading a life directed by anger and resentment based on these past wounds.

Life is unfair. Therefore, we all have compelling reasons to cling to our grudges and animosities. We may feel a great sense of satisfaction and justification in doing so, but we are adversely affected emotionally, spiritually, and physically by holding on to past wounds. Mind-body research reveals a high correlation between anger and depression, cancer, and heart disease.

Additionally, not letting go keeps us prisoners of our past. We are unable to move forward to establish healthy relationships with others, let alone ourselves. We can become extremely self-destructive because of something that someone else did to us or, based on our expectations, we think they did to us. By holding on to past anger—reliving it, thinking about it, obsessing over it—we are never free from it. We give the past injustice power as we perpetuate it many times over. We need to ask, "Does holding on to past wounds hurt the offender or does it continue to punish me?"

By forgiving others we are not condoning their behavior but actually doing something to heal ourselves. Because it's an inner process, forgiving someone does not require that we ever see or talk to that person. The forgiveness can simply be in our hearts. We can forgive, understanding that we are all human and make mistakes. At the same time, we must acknowledge that *we will never forget*—i.e., we will learn from our mistakes.

Forgiveness is an act of love and compassion coming from the heart and directed inward. It allows us to release the pain, emotion, resentment, and attachment to this negative energy to which we have become prisoner. When we forgive, we are doing ourselves a favor. We can now lead an emotionally serene and peaceful life, free from the victim mentality, having healed past and present wounds.

Many of our unresolved wounds come from childhood because we were unable to protect ourselves. As adults, not only can we help heal our past wounds, but we can make sure they will never happen again. When we have been deeply wounded in childhood, the work of forgiveness can take years. The process of healing runs the gamut from grief, rage, sorrow, confusion, and self-hatred to loving, accepting, and forgiving ourselves and others. Finally, we can feel a sense of joy as we free ourselves from being a prisoner in our own heart.

During the time you spend on this healing path it will be helpful to remember some key points:

◇ We need to accept and forgive ourselves—we did the best we could at the time.

◇ Our power lies in our attitude and interpretation. We can change the way we feel about ourselves, another person, or a situation by changing our attitude and viewing life from a different perspective. This will help us ease the pain and release our victim mentality so that we may feel love in our hearts.

◇ When we get hurt, we have choices in how we respond to the situation. We can become angry and carry a grudge, feeling that certain individuals or society are hurting us intentionally. In this mode, we operate as helpless victims. Or, as the following story relates, we commit to seeing good in ourselves and in others—which is reflected in a win-win attitude and a personal, responsible approach to life.

The following is Basha's story, which we hope will clearly illustrate the concept of forgiveness:

To the outside world, I was raised by a father who was fun, always smiling, and very warm and helpful to others. He was loved by everyone. Yet to his children, whom he loved so much, his behavior was critical and judgmental. He had high expectations for our success, hardly ever complimenting us. I felt that I was never good enough for him. There were conditions to his love. He was also upset because we did not share his values and perspectives. He would not take the time to listen and, in turn, did not know or understand us. He felt that his role was to be the breadwinner and part-time disciplinarian. Consequently, he never really spent time with my sister and me because he worked long hours. When he was home he hardly spoke with us. We rarely had family meals together. He spent his time relaxing and playing with our dog, Nikki, a toy poodle, or with my male cousins. (I learned later, when I was able to be an unemotional observer, that he had no idea how to interact with daughters, so he kept his distance.)

For years I felt unlovable and unlikable. I was always trying to get him to love me. I vacillated between misbehaving in areas that were important to him—by acting out in Hebrew school, defiantly leading the class singing "Onward Christian Soldiers"—and being the perfect daughter, getting up every Sunday morning for years to go to work with him in our family business. Nothing I did changed our relationship. I wavered between "beating myself up" and being angry at my father. I always personalized his behavior toward me.

As a teenager, I asked my mother to divorce my father and even went into therapy, trying to get my father to change. Dr. E. kept saying to me, "Basha, the focus needs to be on you making changes. You can't change your father. He's the way he is. It's the best way he knows how to show you his love because of his personal history."

I was enraged! How could a therapist say that it was my problem? Now I was angry not only at my father, but at the male therapist and, in turn, I trusted no men. While dating, I tried unconsciously to work through the issue with my father, alternating between dating really nice men (whom I would not let love me) and critical, cool, aloof men whom I would chase. It never worked when my focus was on getting someone else to love me unconditionally, instead of learning to forgive, love, and accept myself and my father.

About fifteen years ago, I finally acknowledged that not only did I have poor self-esteem but my relationships with men were disastrous. I was devastated! I decided to stop dating and devote my free time to self-healing and forgiveness. I felt to-

tally unlovable, because the way my father tried to show his love did not fit my picture of how a father should love a daughter—the "Father Knows Best" syndrome.

After many years of soul searching, I came to the following truthful, simple, yet deep emotional realization:

I love my father and he'll never be the father that I would have chosen.

And, more important:

My father loves me and I'll never be the daughter
that he would have chosen.

For days I was hysterically crying as I came to forgive us both. I was finally able to let go of my dream of the perfect father and confronted the truth that I could never be the daughter he wanted. Underneath these initially hurtful truths, I experienced real love between us. Within a week, I felt joyful, peaceful, and free. I no longer needed or wanted to change him. I realized that my father was critical of me not because he didn't love me but because his values were different from mine. He could only accept or see his point of view.

I now felt his love, and was able to accept and appreciate him for who he was and what he was able to give me. I was no longer angry at him and finally was able to love him unconditionally, with no expectations. In retrospect, I never realized that I treated my father worse than he treated me. All my father ever wanted was for me to love and accept him unconditionally instead of being angry at him for not meeting my expectations of how a father should behave. I needed to change first because he lacked the skill to do it any differently.

As I changed, his behavior toward me changed. He became the loving father that I had always wanted. By accepting and forgiving both my father and me, a wonderful and fulfilling relationship was born. When I saw the truth, I could make new choices and I no longer needed to sabotage myself anymore. In turn, the type of men that I was now attracted to also changed. I started dating loving, open men whom I could finally be intimate with because I felt worthy and lovable. Forgiveness allowed my personal history to be healed, which changed my whole life.

About six years after we healed our relationship, my father died suddenly. Fortunately, at the time of his death, my father and I were the best of friends. We en-

joyed spending time together. I miss him very much. What comforts me is the continuous presence of his positive, loving energy. The greatest gift that I gave myself is that when my father died, I was at peace with our relationship and felt our mutual love and acceptance.

Six months after my father's death, I met Jeff. I know that my father brought me my wonderful husband. Forgiveness freed me to live in peace and serenity, to discover the father that I always wanted, and to be with my eternal love, my spiritual partner, Jeff.

SOULWORK

This is an opportunity to root out any festering resentments that you have toward family and/or past or present dates and partners. Then you'll have the opportunity to let it all go, if you choose.

1. Make a list of all the reasons and justifications that you give yourself for holding on to anger and resentment. Consider your family-of-origin and current relationships.

2. Write an actual letter to yourself focusing on the areas that you need to forgive yourself for. Remember that you are human and, therefore, you make mistakes. You've held on to this guilt and shame long enough to learn from it. You don't need to punish yourself any longer. You deserve to move on with your life.

3. Make a list of the people that you would like to forgive. Slowly start getting your life back by forgiving them, one at a time. One way is to write each of those people a letter. Whether or not you actually send it or communicate directly with them is irrelevant. Remember, one of the criteria for having a healthy relationship with a partner is to have made peace with your family-of-origin and past relationships. This process is important for you, not for them.

4. Reread Basha's story and reflect on what areas of your life can be benefited by forgiving yourself and another. Remember that forgiveness develops one step at a time. Be gentle and compassionate. Dr. C. Norman Shealy, in *The Self-Healing Workbook*, offers a number of suggestions for

resolving anger, fear, and guilt and for learning to forgive. Consider, for example, Day 18 in his book:

Feel good to yourself by resolving unfinished business. Recall any significant past hurt—anger, fear, guilt. Be aware of how it feels. Note exactly where you feel the stress. And ask yourself these questions:

◇ Is there anything I can do now to correct the situation?

◇ Can I discuss the hurt with the person responsible and ask them to apologize? Can I sue them?

◇ Have I found a way to avoid ever having such a problem again?

◇ What did I learn from that problem that makes me a better person?

◇ Am I willing to accept and forgive the person(s) involved?

◇ If not, what will it take for me to forgive?

◇ Does it make me feel good to hold a grudge?

◇ Can it solve the problem if I continue to be upset?

◇ Am I willing to resolve my anger, fear, or guilt in order to feel good?

MEDITATION

I am committed to working on forgiving myself and others. I know that as I continue to work on forgiveness, especially of my parents, it will bring me peace as well as the freedom to find the life and soul partner that will love and nurture me.

Soulwork Step 4:
Embrace the Shadow

11

The path toward wholeness and consciousness involves embracing what Carl Jung calls our shadow. The shadow part of our personality encompasses hidden, negative behaviors and experiences. We are all a combination of both good and bad attributes, and it's the balance we maintain between the two that defines who we are as a person.

Maintaining good self-esteem entails living consciously by recognizing our faults, or shadow parts, and avoiding self-denial by courageously acknowledging and embracing who we are. This process encourages our personal healing and wholeness. We also need to encourage others to embrace these ideas. Mutual acceptance and intimacy is a major component in the journey toward soul mate or spiritual partnership.

Most of us, however, have a very difficult time accepting what we label as the dark parts of ourselves. We believe that we need to be perfect to be loved. We attempt to keep secrets from ourselves and others in the hope that we can avoid dealing with our shadow parts. We often deny our anger, selfishness, and addictive behaviors as well as our other negative qualities in order to avoid confronting our limitations or showing our vulnerability.

The facade we create is supported by our strong network of defense mechanisms. By living in illusion, we cannot see ourselves clearly. We deny our negative inner qualities and impulses by saying such things to ourselves as:

◇ "It's no big deal, no one will notice."
◇ "Let it slide, I'll do it better next time."
◇ Because she didn't act right, I feel this way" (victim mentality).

At the same time we can easily see these negative qualities in others. In addition, the qualities that we do not acknowledge in ourselves, we project onto other people. We are hypocrites! Whenever we find ourselves saying the previous statements or criticizing others, we can be sure that we are protecting ourselves with self-sustaining illusions, instead of seeing the truth concerning our own behavior.

The spiritual practice of embracing our shadow involves accepting our good and bad attributes. This is one reason why admission of sins or sincere acknowledgment of shortcomings is such a necessary part of every spiritual path. We are here on earth to make mistakes and learn lessons. We are not perfect. The shadow lives in our snubs, criticisms, snide remarks, grudges, lies, pettiness, procrastination, and self-pity. We need to recognize them without judgment.

We also must accept that these are areas we need to improve. We're always in the process of becoming better. When our shadow rears its ugly head, we must deal with it by addressing the issue directly. We know deep down inside that even though it may seem much easier to live in illusion, or to blame our mood on outside circumstances, such behavior is ultimately destructive to ourselves and to the possibility of a healthy relationship.

The full and joyful acceptance of the worst in ourselves is the only way to transform our shadow because what we resist, persists. This acceptance is the path of inner truth and freedom. We don't have to hide; we can acknowledge and take responsibility for everything—the good, the bad, and the ugly. Otherwise we're living behind walls, protecting ourselves and criticizing others so that no one can see who we truly are.

Part of loving ourselves fully is to face our demons and learn from them. We need to understand what we are avoiding and hiding, what frightens us and causes us hurt, that is seeking expression. We must become an objective observer of ourselves and be fully accountable for our actions or we will find ourselves in the same difficult situation over and over again. We must start looking at the negative things within ourselves in a different way in order to see them clearly.

Negative habits can be transformed through self-observation. Such observation, taking place impartially and without judgment, may help change how we feel. This level of self-awareness makes our personal problems more transparent. We become more responsive to our feelings, focusing attention on light and healing. This newfound vulnerability encourages the alignment of our soul and personality.

Envy, for example, which usually resides in our shadow, affords us the opportunity for growth if it is brought to consciousness and used for self-transformation. Take the case of Gloria who was very envious of her best friend Martha. When things were not going well with Martha in the dating arena, Gloria was solicitous and close, ready to help in any way. However, when Martha had a loving boyfriend, Gloria became critical and uncommunicative and put her friendship with Martha in jeopardy. The possibility of losing her relationship with Martha forced Gloria to examine her envy and confront it. She discovered that envy was truly a gift that helped her to understand something about herself. She realized that she was envious of Martha because she wanted what Martha had. This realization gave her a new awareness of her value system and what she wanted in her relationships. Gloria was able to let go of her envy and was now ready for a loving man in her life. As Gloria's example reveals, when the wisdom of the shadow teaches us to see the beauty that lies within, we can touch the heart and soul of another.

SOULWORK

Unearthing the shadow side of ourselves can be difficult, but necessary, work to get you on the path to soul mate or spiritual partnership.

1. Which individuals do you criticize the most? Look at yourself honestly. Are these the qualities that are hard for you to accept in yourself?

2. To become an effective self-observer, simply watch yourself in action several times during the day, observing what you assess as your positive and negative qualities with an impartial eye. Don't make any judgments, just make observations. This practice is much harder than it sounds.

3. If this practice is too difficult, don't become discouraged. Learn to meditate! The purpose of meditating is to calm your mind by observing thoughts and feelings passing through while you keep returning to a particular mantra (sound) or your breath. The premise is to remain

unattached from your thoughts. This refocusing on a particular sound or your breath prevents the train of thought or judgments from taking over.

4. Make a list of the qualities that you like about yourself as well as the qualities that you are uncomfortable with or dislike. Observe the judgments that arise.

5. Be vulnerable as you share intimately with a close friend the qualities that you like about yourself as well as the shadow parts of you.

6. Listen while the same friend tells you about who you are, sharing your good and not-so-good qualities. Remember that this person loves you despite knowing the good, the bad, and the ugly. You don't need to be perfect to be loved.

MEDITATION

I am committed to embracing all the parts of me so that I can fully love myself and become the best possible me.

Soulwork Step 5:
Feel, Heal, and Move On

12

All of our feelings are integral parts of the human experience. They need to be respected and honored. Yet many of us have experienced so much pain in our lives that we have virtually shut down our emotions. We often do not know how we feel because we are so out of touch with some parts of ourselves.

In order to survive, we have denied our feelings of guilt, anger, sadness, and fear as well as joy, exhilaration, and excitement. Our hearts are so shut down that we are unable to experience, let alone express, either pleasure or pain. We become the living dead. Therefore, many of us are frightened and uncomfortable with the prospect of doing deep emotional work. Our fear is that doing so would involve digging up old buried feelings, memories, and pain. It's easier to maintain the status quo, which feels like we're running in place, going nowhere. However, by confronting risk we may finally address these feelings and acquire the life as well as the partner we deserve.

In order to be in a soul mate or spiritual partnership you must be committed to authentically communicating your feelings and concerns to your partner. This includes sharing your past emotional wounds and your family history, and how they affect your ability to interact with another in a healthy manner. This openness allows your partner not to take your behavior personally, so that he or she can help you heal and grow.

About ten years ago Basha was in a soul mate relationship with a very nurturing and supportive man named Julian. In one of their discussions, she shared that she was sad because she had no idea how to express anger and fight fairly. When her parents were angry, her father would scream and criticize while her mother would withdraw and not speak. There was never any resolution. Basha stated naively to Julian, "I know that I don't know how to fight fairly; however, I can promise you that I won't withdraw like my mother did." A few days later Julian and Basha had a fight and Basha immediately turned her back on him. Julian, lovingly and with compassion, tapped her shoulder and said, "Look what you just did." Basha immediately broke into tears, realizing that she'd automatically behaved just like her mother. No matter how much she wanted to do it differently, this was the only behavior she was familiar with. Her wounded child had automatically protected itself by withdrawing, assuming that she would be rejected because of the conflict.

Because Basha had taken the risk and shared her fears and history with Julian, he did not take her behavior personally, since he was doing his own healing work. Therefore, he began to teach her the art of fighting fairly. In turn, Basha started to trust that she would not be rejected by the people she loved, solely because she disagreed with them.

What we need to understand to make us less fearful of working on our past is that we cannot heal our feelings. Feelings are simply information that tell us what is going on inside. They are a reflection of how we interpret the world. Every thought, belief, and assumption that we make affects how we feel; yet we learn most of these beliefs from our "tribe" and society, and they color our automatic interpretation of life. Acknowledging and accepting our feelings is necessary in order to be able to live in the moment and experience life as it comes, with no prejudgments or false expectations.

If we want to change the way we feel, we must first change our attitudes and beliefs, which are at the root of how and why we feel a certain way. Our attitude about life needs healing. Therefore, healing painful memories and releasing them can occur by changing our perception of the stories we tell ourselves. Our reality is totally dependent on our interpretation of facts.

Denial, like all defenses, works superficially for a while. Healing begins when we realize that the energy of those negative feelings has become trapped inside our bodies and is doing us more harm than good. Suffering is due entirely to clinging to the past or resisting change. It is a sign of our unwillingness to move on in life. We need to ask ourselves, "Would I rather understand my anger and underlying sadness and not have it control me, or would I rather be unaware of it and have it dominate my life?"

We all have the opportunity to write a new life's script for ourselves. Anne, a forty-three-year-old attorney, chose to do exactly that. She originally thought of herself as a fearful, invisible caterpillar. As she changed her interpretation of life, she metamorphosed into a beautiful butterfly. Her story is an inspiration to us all.

The important thing is to know yourself, slow down and take the time to reflect. I stopped defending myself against what I imagined other people were thinking about me. The phrase I kept repeating to myself is: "What other people say, do, think, and believe is about them, about their values, not about me." Accepting and internalizing this concept allowed me to step out and be noticed.

It all started last fall when I finally decided to quit smoking, not for health reasons but for personal visibility. I came to the realization that cigarette smoke repulses even me and that most people dismiss smokers immediately. All they see is smoke. They don't see the person behind the smoke because they find it so repulsive. Smoking was just another way I was hiding "me" from the world. Quitting smoking represented a real longing to stop hiding and to start living my life.

I quit a few days ahead of schedule. As hard as it was, I never doubted that I would be successful. I felt like an invading army was attacking and defeating the cigarettes. I knew I was going to win this time. My attitude was different.

This process started me thinking about other ways that I've maintained my invisibility. I had grown up with a childish, passive attitude about life. I never thought about what I really wanted to do or what I had to contribute to others. Instead, I was always so grateful when people would be nice to me. Even if they acted jerky, I would accept it. I retreated from people who genuinely wanted to be friends because I was afraid that they would have demanded something that wasn't there. I thought of myself as a small child trying to live an adult's life. I didn't know who I was, what I liked, or actually what I was about.

For me, becoming visible was coming home to myself. I realized that I had been trying to define myself by what I imagined other people thought and felt because I had not come to terms with my own identity. What had been missing from my life was someone at home, inside, calling the shots.

Even though I don't know where becoming visible is going to lead, I am committed to being authentic and revealing myself to others. I now say to myself, "one step at a time" or "one day at a time," and I fight the individual battles inside me until I get where I want to be.

It's not frightening anymore to live as a nonsmoker and be visible. Even if people judge me, I keep saying to myself that I cannot forfeit my life so other people's insecurities can be assuaged. It's not right for me or for them. People have to face their fears, like I keep doing every day. If they choose not to, that's a choice that they've made, like I've chosen to face mine. I still struggle to be honest with people. It's not easy. I hate conflict or arguments. However, I have committed myself to honesty and becoming visible in every realm of my life.

What has made the process so easy is that for the first time, someone is home. It finally feels like my small wounded child has a protective and loving mother, someone to take care of her. For the first time in my life I feel very secure and happy. I feel like I'm not so separated from myself and, in turn, the world.

Feeling gives us the freedom to invent ourselves, to free the prisoners of our past. When we are numb to our feelings, we lose contact with who we are and can't feel joy. Identifying and coming to terms with your emotions and feelings might feel strange and scary at first. Be gentle. Initially, it will probably be quite difficult for those of you who were criticized for expressing feelings or never saw any type of model for this behavior. It can also be uncomfortable for those who are used to experiencing life mostly through the thinking perspective. You will experience many types of feelings as you allow past hurts to surface, including anger, confusion, and frustration. Sometimes we feel worse before we feel better.

The healing process needs to start slowly and carefully. We must come to grips with the various aspects of learning to experience these feelings in our own time frame.

⬦ Find a safe place in your home or elsewhere that you can enjoy privacy and solitude (with no interruptions).

⬦ Give yourself the time to listen to your feelings and the reasons behind them. Put them in writing if it is helpful.

⬦ Stay in touch with what you are feeling by slowing down, focusing on remaining conscious.

◊ What we believe about ourselves determines how we feel about the world around us. To heal shame we must realize that it's only an interpretation we have made concerning ourselves. It's not until we challenge this belief that it loses its power over us.

◊ To accelerate the healing process we must let go of past perceptions and accept only the present moment as real. We must see the past as something that happened, and is over now. Now we can invent a new interpretation of ourselves as well as reframe our history.

◊ We have feelings, but we are not our feelings.

◊ Be able to communicate honestly what you are feeling, to yourself and at least one other person. In the beginning, just acknowledging your feelings and telling your story is essential to the healing process.

◊ Whether it's a friend or a therapist we choose to share our feelings and stories with, that person must be warm, compassionate, accepting, and caring. He or she has to be comfortable with the expression of all emotions. He or she must value sharing feelings and have an awareness of his or her own history.

◊ Emotional intimacy means allowing safe people to see and be with the real you.

As the process of acknowledging and accepting our feelings continues, we begin to experience a strong sense of empowerment as we gradually come home to ourselves (as Anne did) and no longer let our fears run our lives. Our feelings will automatically support us. As we change our interpretation of our past history, we can then begin to heal the past and invent a new future. We can trust our feelings as they align with our new ways of viewing the world. We need to learn to love and be compassionate to ourselves and others.

SOULWORK

Remember to find a safe, comfortable place to explore your feelings.

1. If it is difficult for you to feel, the first step is to breathe deeply. Pay attention to what thoughts and feelings come up without judging or censoring.

2. It is essential to stay in touch with the joys in your life and to remember what makes you happy. Every night, make a list of what you feel grateful for and what joys were presented during that day. *Simple Abundance,* by Sarah Ban Breathnach, provides eloquent examples.

3. Each day, jot down your feelings about a particular situation—either positive or negative. What point of view have you taken? To see another perspective, write the same scenario, looking at it objectively and referring to yourself as "he" or "she." Think about other possible interpretations—discuss them with others. Observe how your feelings change as your interpretation changes.

4. During times when feelings take you on a roller-coaster ride, rather than blocking them, study these emotions and attempt to understand them. Then try to replace these feelings with thoughts or a new interpretation that will aid in your soul's development. What new meaning can you give this experience?

5. Learn to be aware of certain interpersonal relationships and situations that are unsafe. Either stay away or prepare yourself (thus healing the child, as Anne did), by saying to yourself, "When other people's words hurt me, I practice forgiveness and compassion. I will make a conscious effort. When other people are criticizing me it really has to do with their own pain, needs, and fears. I have been there myself and need to be gentle with them and not respond in kind. I am no longer angry at life by taking everything so personally.

MEDITATION

I am committed to healing myself by experiencing my feelings and expressing them to emotionally safe people. This will prepare me to be intimate, loving, and authentic with my soul partner.

Soulwork Step 6:
Attain a Balanced Life

13

It's not always possible to fall in love or win a promotion every time we need a positive stroke. However, it is possible to boost our health and happiness quotient, smooth out the ups and downs of life, and make the most of who we are by making sure that we get enough of the "being" things in life. Therefore, we need to be in charge of directing and designing how we lead our lives every day.

A being activity is defined as time spent pursuing something for no other reason than that it supports, nurtures, and helps us rejuvenate, while keeping us connected to our inner values and higher self. These activities touch our heart, soul, and spirit when, for example, we connect with another on a meaningful level. Participating in being activities perpetuates our sense of wholeness and of loving ourselves.

In order to maintain a soulful connection, both partners must cherish time spent just being. This lifestyle choice enhances their ability to remain conscious so they can choose nurturing activities together. This supports the alignment of the soul and personality which is essential in any soulful partnership. Remember, each person in a soul mate relationship must value becoming a whole and complete person. Reinventing the we together entails valuing authenticity, sharing and communicating honest feelings, and participating in being as well as doing activities alone and together.

The following is a guide to the categories of being activities that we need to include in our daily lives to ensure that we are taking care of our total self—body, mind, and spirit. Thus, no matter what's going on in our lives, we feel good about ourselves because we can control these areas.

Spirituality/Meaningfulness—devoting time to an activity that is personally significant and meaningful and helps us stay connected with our higher self. Some examples are meditating, praying, practicing tai chi, reading a contemplative book, or walking in nature.

Intimacy/Communication—specifically setting aside time for being connections. This encompasses taking time in which the focus is getting to know ourselves better as well as sharing intimately and vulnerably with another. Some examples are journaling, sharing feelings with a dear friend, or going to therapy.

Sleep—getting between seven and nine hours of good, deep sleep. The number of hours we sleep depends on our own body clock, so we need to listen to our internal signals telling us when we are tired. Sleep is very healing. It is the time when our body rejuvenates itself, through both rest and dreams. It's our everyday vacation. A well-rested body can face the everyday stress of life.

Idle Time—the leisure time that we designate every day for an activity that has no purpose other than enjoyment. There is no goal. It's not being lazy— as we often negatively say of ourselves. It is our time to participate in activities that nurture and rejuvenate us simply because we enjoy ourselves while doing them. Idle-time activities include talking on the phone, window shopping, attending sporting events, or reading a novel.

Relaxation—an activity where every part of you is relaxed, especially your mind. It's hard to live joyfully and peacefully when the weight of the world is on your shoulders. Part of the relaxing experience is to create a private retreat that is designated for healing and relaxation. The ambiance needs to be familiar, nurturing, undisturbed, and peaceful. Some examples of relaxation are getting a massage, meditating, using guided imagery, listening to classical music, or taking a bubble bath.

Pleasurable—an activity at which we know we will succeed almost 100 percent of the time. Success in this context means that during the activity we feel good about ourselves and feel warm and nurtured inside. We experience love for ourselves and others while we smile and are at peace. These activities are especially important because most things in life don't give us pleasure; they are based on the shoulds dictated by our families, jobs, or culture. The length of the activity is not as important as our intention to participate in something that is pleasurable for us, even for five minutes in our hectic day. It is important to feel certain of the outcome. Some examples are talking to a best friend, drinking a leisurely cup of cappuccino at our favorite cafe, getting a hug from someone we love, or petting our animal.

Play—any activity that tends to produce feelings of joy while having fun. While participating in the activity, we smile, joke, and laugh. Feeling joyful and happy increases our positive attitude about ourselves and the world, encouraging our creativity. Some examples of play are going to the movies, participating in sports, going to an amusement park, playing cards, or playing with animals or children.

Each of the following two categories can be either a doing or a being activity depending on the attitude we adopt concerning our motivation and goal for engaging in them:

Eating—part of loving ourselves is eating consciously and choosing healthy foods because we want premium fuel for our bodies. We need to remain conscious about the time and place that we select for this nurturing activity.

Exercise—a physical activity that increases our body strength, improves our cardiovascular fitness, and focuses on endurance, balance, and flexibility in various forms. We can participate in one or several activities as long as we really enjoy them and do them correctly. The goal is to turn our physical fitness efforts into a form of reverence and gratitude for life as well as a way to create, through our body, deeper connections with ourselves, nature, and those around us. Some examples are hiking, jogging, weight training, tennis, low-impact aerobics, dancing, and yoga.

We all need to participate in being activities to replenish ourselves. They keep us balanced because so much of our time is spent in doing activities and expending energy out in the world. The question we need to ask ourselves is which of the above being activities do we include in our typical, too short day?

When Jane asked herself this question, she realized that she only participated in hurried doing activities except for sleep and idleness. Her daily schedule consisted only of exercise, sleeping, eating, and working. The rest of her day was devoted to idleness in order to escape from life. In essence, her life revolved around doing, not being. All the activities she participated in focused on shoulds—staying thin, dating wealthy men, maintaining a dissatisfying career as an attorney, and fulfilling other people's expectations. She had lost herself and given up her dreams, to meet other people's approval. No wonder she felt anxious, burnt out, tired, and needy and was looking for a man to take her away from her empty existence.

Jane, like almost all the clients we've counseled and coached, realized that her life was not balanced. She needed to reclaim herself. After her discovery, she purposefully chose to leave the fast lane, slow down her life, and devote time to discovering what was meaningful and joyful. In this way, she learned what things she enjoyed, based on who she is rather than what she did. She realized that self-love supports her being and doing natures by creating a balanced life, in which her needs and wants in both arenas are addressed.

While being is important, the following categories are the two doing activities that must be included in a balanced life:

Work—all the activities that we need and have to do every day for ourselves and others; not just our nine-to-five job. Some examples of work are going to the dentist, going food shopping and cooking as an obligation, even brushing our teeth. Having a productive life means successfully completing the many activities that we have to do, not necessarily what we want to do. As a matter of fact, if we observe our lives, the majority of time is spent in this realm.

Planning—sitting down to consciously plan the weekly activities that support our lives in every area—physical, spiritual, and emotional—taking into consideration doing and being activities. This process involves asking ourselves, "Who am I?" and "What am I?" and "What action will support me at this time?" Many activities, depending on our attitude, can meet our needs. For example, Jeff, Basha's husband, loves tennis. His experience while playing tennis encompasses the realms of pleasure, exercise, and play. He turned what is a doing activity for most people into a being event.

Depending on our perspective and attitude, any activity can mean different things to us at different times, which Kathy discovered while doing this exercise. When she had leisure time, shopping became a being activity, especially when she went with one of her best friends and had no particular goal. Shopping became a rewarding adventure, chock-full of pleasure, play, idleness, intimacy, and communication. On the other hand, when she had to buy something specific, within a particular time frame, the same shopping activity became a chore and, in turn, work.

SOULWORK

Before you can fill your time with being activities you need to determine how you spend your time.

1. Look at your typical day. What activities take up your time? What percentage of time do you spend on being activities?

2. If you could have a life that fulfilled all your dreams, what would it look like? Would there be more being activities included every day? Think about the positives and negatives as you ponder this question. How would your life be affected today with these changes in place?

3. Consider the nine being activities on pages 77–78. Under each of these categories, list various activities that you would enjoy spending time on, that would nurture you. Also list those you might be interested in exploring.

4. Below is a three-day sample of our Creative Structure Weekly Planner that follow the list of being and doing activities previously described. After reading the instructions, write down in the sample three-day plan specific activities that would support who you *desire* to become.

Enjoy the discovery process. Beginning new habits is never the challenge. It's sticking to a new lifestyle that supports loving ourselves and becoming whole that is difficult. We are creatures of habit and have a hard time changing, even when it is beneficial. What better gift can you offer yourself than following the Creative Structure Weekly Planner design to create a personalized schedule? Because you are inventing a new life, you should use a pencil with an eraser. Don't worry about making changes in the schedule. That's what life is about. It takes at least ninety days to learn a new behavior. You will probably make many mistakes along the way because you are not used to focusing on beingness and who you are.

A typical weekly plan should minimally include the following:

EVERY DAY	EVERY OTHER DAY
Eating	Idle Time
Sleep	Relaxation
Pleasure	Exercise
Planning	Play
Intimacy/Communication	Spirituality/Meaningfulness
Work	

You should also provide a period of free time in your schedule for breakdowns or unexpected emergencies. Always be prepared for change.

Refer to the list above to create a three-day schedule on the time chart, including both being and doing activities—and breakdown time—in the three days.

Afterward, consider the schedule you've created. Would following this plan help you bring your life more into balance? How would leading a balanced life support you in seeking a soul mate or spiritual partnership?

CREATIVE STRUCTURE WEEKLY PLANNER			
	Sunday	Monday	Tuesday
7 a.m.			
8 a.m.			
9 a.m.			
10 a.m.			
11 a.m.			
12 p.m.			
1 p.m.			
2 p.m.			
3 p.m.			
4 p.m.			
5 p.m.			
6 p.m.			
7 p.m.			
8 p.m.			
9 p.m.			
10 p.m.			
11 p.m.			

MEDITATION

I love myself enough to devote time to creating and living a Creative Structure Daily Plan that supports who I am as well as what I am.

Soulwork Step 7: Become the Best Possible You

14

"Perfection is not for human beings, perfection is for angels."

—RABBI REUVEN BULKA

The pursuit of perfection is a trap. Our refusal to accept of this truth creates much frustration and suffering in our lives. As we consider our humanity, we must realize that there is no such condition as absolute perfection. Our goal is to achieve excellence in those areas of our lives that we value and to which we are committed. To achieve fulfillment, you must be and become the best possible you.

Many of us were raised to believe perfection is possible, so we continue to chase this unattainable goal. Following are some issues we should consider regarding the pursuit of perfection:

⬦ We are not good at everything. Nor can we be instantly good at new tasks. We need to be forgiving of ourselves as we take on something new.

⬦ We will never be happy with ourselves or others if we only value the end result. Fulfillment in life means valuing all the steps along the way, honoring the process toward a goal.

⬦ The perfectionist operates only in the doing mode, never loving himself completely. Anything less than perfection is unacceptable to him.

⬦ Perfectionists believe they are only as good as their last victory. They can never be truly happy with themselves unless they keep on performing. With this point of view, when they stop performing, their sense of self-worth is totally diminished. Not only do they love themselves with conditions, but because they have not valued who they are, they feel empty.

The driving motivation for us all is self-esteem, which has to do not only with how we feel about ourselves, accepting all our parts, but also with how we live in the world effectively. While striving for excellence, we need to create a realistic human standard for ourselves and others based on grounded and practical conditions of satisfaction. Excellence means that we accept, without judgment, the areas we excel in as well as those we do not. In those deficient areas, we need to learn new behaviors and skills in order to be able to take effective action; or we need to accept the deficiencies and find another means of handling the problem.

For example, Howard is very competent at being organized but is computer illiterate. This simple assessment contains no judgment; it is based on observation of his ability to take effective action in these two domains. It's not good or bad, it just is. Some things we do well, others we do not. Assuming this attitude, we will be able to embrace both our skills and limitations in a healthy, balanced, and integrated manner. If learning the computer is an essential skill for Howard to possess, he must first declare himself a beginner and find an excellent coach to teach him to become competent on the computer.

We can't be all things to all people, including ourselves. We are both teachers and students. We must learn enough about our abilities and deficiencies in order to accept what we can do, what we must learn to do, and what we can delegate to others. Self-knowledge is essential in determining how we operate and in what areas we need help. Becoming the best possible you recognizes these aspects and focuses on those areas where you can achieve successfully, rather than on those where you can't.

No matter what our level of competence, there is always more to do. If we get caught in the vicious cycle of feeling like an underdog, we will always be angry and resentful. In addition, by procrastinating, we will eventually beat ourselves up over what we should have done. Reality shows us that the more we acknowledge our abilities, the more we will naturally want to do and learn, especially in areas that might be risky. We will be rewarded by taking the risk and stimulated to take on more.

However, we must recognize that the skills that make us successful in business may be far different from those needed to be an excellent parent and spouse. Being an expert in one area does not necessarily support competence in a different realm. Take the example of a stereotypical CEO of a large company. She may have organizational prowess and the ability to intuitively guide the company's long-term objectives, but the same person might have difficulty tending to the needs of her daughter and husband. Different qualities are needed to nurture those relationships and, although an expert and master in business, she needs to learn different skills to be successful in her family life.

Being vulnerable is a great asset for every individual in specific situations. Our CEO might need help from her family, even though she is a great leader at work. Experts can become vulnerable by adopting the beginner mentality. This new attitude encourages authenticity and the ability to interact with others and life fully. This process allows us to stretch while we depend on others for support, becoming more compassionate and patient, learning to value others for their skills and abilities. Since soul mate and spiritual partner relationships value learning, growth, and change, this beginner's attitude is essential in achieving a successful and nurturing partnership.

Soul mate relationships are the perfect opportunity to learn the relationship skills required for the qualities of compassion, the ability to love unconditionally, sensitivity to the needs of others, generosity, sincerity, and honesty. For spiritual partnership, excellence is required in all these areas. These virtues are seen when, in partnership, we are able to keep promises to each other and maintain open communication. Nurturing relationships are based on a mutual sense of reverence and admiration. We respect people for their consistency of performance in areas that matter to us as individuals. We admire people for their excellent moral qualities. These virtues must both be present for transcendence to spiritual partnership. That's why it's essential for each of us to complete our own internal preparation, to fully love and embrace ourselves, before we are ready to begin the search for our soul relationship.

If I'm not for myself,
Who will be?
If I'm for myself only,
What am I?
If not now, when?

—HILLEL

Valuing both the human being as well as the human doing is essential in becoming the best possible you. This process is integral to the alignment of our soul and personality. Having a nurturing and successful relationship with ourselves allows us to achieve excellence in different arenas. Being able to ask for help and allow our partner to support us is the give-and-take necessary to be in a soulful partnership.

SOULWORK

How can you be your best? Take some time to let go of perfectionism and acknowledge your areas of expertise and competence.

1. What is standing between the life you have and the life you want? What are the roadblocks that prevent you from making changes?

2. Are you a perfectionist with yourself and others? What benefits do you derive from this perspective? What liabilities occur from operating in this mode, especially in the area of intimacy and partnership?

3. Consider the extent of perfection you expect in your life. Make a list of your areas of excellence. Next, list the areas in which you are incompetent or a beginner. Try to be impartial, with no false modesty. Show this list to a close friend and objectively share your feelings. Be open to feedback.

4. In what areas would it benefit you to learn new skills, showing up as a beginner? Consider specifically the areas that relate to the virtues that are essential for soul mate or spiritual partnership, such as trust or intimacy. Why would it benefit you to learn these skills? How has the lack of these skills sabotaged your past relationships? Think of someone you trust who could help you improve one of these skills. Ask that person for help and be prepared to assess your progress. Remember, every skill can be learned, including effective partnership attributes.

5. Spend a few minutes at the end of each day focusing on your daily experiences, both good and bad. What lessons were presented relating to becoming the best possible you? End your evening contemplating your blessings and being thankful for your gifts.

MEDITATION

I am committed to becoming the best possible me. I acknowledge the areas that I excel in and respect and honor what I need to learn, especially in the area of intimacy and partnership. Life is about making mistakes and learning from them. Being in a soul mate or spiritual partnership is the culmination of leading a life that supports both who I am and what I do. This is my path.

The Relationship
Continuum

Companion➜➜➜➜Soul Mate ➜➜➜➜Spiritual Partner

15

Now that you have completed the work on yourself, you are ready to embark on the journey toward a soulful relationship. First you must consider the type of relationship that you want. The three types of healthy relationships are companionship, soul mate, and spiritual partnership (We call these relationships mateable). No one type is necessarily better than the others. When you consciously choose one, it indicates that this category of relationship supports who and what you are and best represents your values.

Companionship, soul mate, and spiritual partnership exist on a continuum, but if you achieve the first level—companionship—you don't automatically progress to the second and third. Companionship does not place you on a spiritual path, but soul mate and spiritual partner do.

If you're unsure about what type of relationship you desire, think about how you feel about change and personal growth. The more you value these in your life, the more likely it is you possess the attitude and qualities to have a soul mate or spiritual partner relationship.

Once you've decided on the type of relationship you want, remember that you're not in a relationship alone. You must keep in mind that although you've done your psycho-spiritual work, you can't drag a partner along who has not done his or her work. It won't happen. The type of relationship you have will depend on the work each of you has done and is willing to do. One way or another, you both need to be roughly at the same level for any of the three types of relationships to be fulfilling.

Along the relationship continuum you may find yourself in different places during your life, probably with different partners, excluding spiritual partnership, which we believe is a lifelong commitment.

COMPANIONSHIP

This relationship generally reflects traditional marriages or relationships. Companions value keeping life on an even keel with minimal change and prefer interactions that take place on a logical rather than a feeling level. Gender roles are clearly defined while external needs such as safety, security, and consistency are maintained.

Companions don't spend the time, energy, and work necessary to invent the we, and therefore both partners remain separate, keeping their I's apart. Another companion scenario occurs where one I becomes passive, giving up his or her identity for the sake of maintaining the status quo of the relationship.

Companions enjoy romantic friendship at the personality level (though not in the emotional or spiritual realm) and usually have mutual respect and admiration. What binds them is a commonality of values (family/tribal), interests, and activities. Whether married or not, living together or apart, they express affection and appreciation for each other. They make a commitment to spend time together with the focus on doing rather than being activities.

Communication between companions is mostly on a personality level. What's missing is the deeper involvement with one's self and in each other. Because companions mainly interpret life through the five senses, they talk about external subjects together but hold back when it comes to issues that are emotionally and spiritually charged. As comfortable and secure as the relationship might be, it's static and rarely broadens or deepens to the point where emotional intimacy occurs. Since companions aren't committed to consciously helping each other learn and grow, they may go outside the relationship to get their emotional and spiritual needs met. They often lead separate lives, spending time either doing things alone or with their own friends.

Power struggles occur frequently in companionship. Living as two separate I's, each person takes a stand that relates to being right, arguing highly personalized issues. It's also not unusual for companions to deal with power struggles by ignoring the core issues and pretending they don't exist. They hope problems will just go away and are afraid or unwilling to rock the boat by confronting them.

Companions may live one or more of the Seven Spiritual Wisdoms, but they live them on an individual rather than a partnership level. They may have balance and meaningfulness in their lives but it's for them alone, not valued as part of their primary relationship. Because companions don't value sharing the Seven Spiritual Wisdoms with another person, the possibility for creating a solid we remains dormant.

Companionship primarily concerns the personality. People in these relationships have usually made a decision (though it may be an unconscious one) not to be on a psychospiritual path. There is nothing wrong with this choice, but people should be aware that if this is what they decide, there is no "natural" progression from this place to a soulful relationship. Unless each partner embraces the Seven Spiritual Wisdoms and does some inner work, they will remain at this level indefinitely.

For many people, companionship represents a good, safe, comfortable relationship. It is the easiest of the three relationships because the partners do not deal with meaningful issues together and are satisfied with meeting each other's needs solely on a personality level. For some couples, this is fine. It is all they are capable of, want, or need. For them a companionship relationship is perfect.

A companion relationship becomes troubled when one person decides to engage in activities that will advance his or her personal growth, while the other person remains content with the status quo. Although love is present, the relationship no longer satisfies that person's need for emotional and spiritual intimacy. At this point, a soulful connection is needed and the old relationship will no longer be viable. When this occurs, the couple has a major decision to make. They must decide either to get on the spiritual path together, to remain together with one person feeling empty and unfulfilled, or to separate.

Gail wrote the following letter to her close friend Janie. In this letter she wrestled with the issues inherent in a relationship where she was on a soul path while her partner was perfectly comfortable in companionship.

Dear Janie,

You're not home tonight and I really needed to talk, so I'm just going to write down my thoughts. . . .

My life again has shifted dramatically, and as I have done many times before, I've started questioning my life, including my relationship with Bob.

As you know, my dad was such a wonderful model for what I want in a man, and in many ways Bob reminds me of him. Bob is a man of loyalty and integrity who values family, friends, and giving back to the community. He doesn't display needy behavior and is extremely self-sufficient, spending long periods of time at peace with himself. He appreciates and respects me and shows his affection and admiration. There's a lot to like and love about him.

So why over the years have I felt restless within myself and the relationship? And why do I feel there's something missing?

Certainly, much of the responsibility lies with me. Stuck in my anger at what I felt was missing, I have been afraid to be totally straightforward and honest about my feelings, burying my emotions rather than confronting them. Afraid, if I was honest, he would be critical or judgmental or—worse yet—go away.

And yet, every time I've told him I wanted a deeper, more authentic relationship, he basically said that my dissatisfaction was my problem, and he was happy with what we had, and wasn't going to spend time changing what he felt was already a good relationship.

It reminds me of that old joke: "How many therapists does it take to screw in a light bulb? Only one, but the light bulb has got to really want to change." Bob never really wants to change.

So, I have again started asking questions of myself. Am I living the type of life that has meaning and purpose? What am I going to do to contribute to a greater good? And, how am I going to come to terms with a man I like and love, but who doesn't have the same vision of an intimate relationship?

I've often thought that our time together seems to run on parallel tracks. At times we come together through family, friends, vacations, and interests to form a single track, only to divide again and continue on separately.

Recently, I asked Bob to picture working on our relationship as a door about to be opened. "Ask yourself," I said, "what are your fears if I open this door? Facing emotional issues? Confrontation? Enmeshment?" Then I suggested he replace that question with another. "What wonderful things could happen if I open this door? The possibility of greater intimacy? New experiences? A stronger connection to myself and the woman I love?"

In the meantime, as he stands in front of the unopened door, I continue to long for more and live with the questions.

SOUL MATE

When most people say they want a soul mate relationship, they don't realize what this truly means because our society uses this term so casually and all-inclusively. In reality, this relationship takes a great amount of courage and requires a lot of work because both partners must have embarked on the psychospiritual path before they meet.

Sheri's story gives us an inspiring example of a woman who has courageously fought her way through life. Her process of becoming conscious encouraged her to face her losses, heal through inner work, and reap the rewards of a soul mate relationship.

Twenty years ago, you could never imagine Sheri being in a healthy, loving relationship. A soul mate relationship was not even a remote possibility. Sheri was raised by a mother who lacked parenting skills and who had a hard time coping with life. Her often absent father was critical, controlling, and emotionally abusive when he was at home. He eventually divorced Sheri's mom and married her best friend when Sheri was nine years old. Sheri's mom couldn't cope, and this left Sheri saddled with the major responsibility of caring for her younger brother Sandy as well as herself. She learned at a young age to be self-reliant and to push down her emotions and feelings because she had no one to depend on. Her only release was to cry when she was alone.

Sheri survived by becoming the family rebel, while her brother took on the role of the good and favorite child. She acted out by drinking, experimenting with drugs, observing no curfew, and refusing to go to school. She was always in a power struggle with her family, especially her father, who was equally headstrong. However, because of her fighting spirit, she graduated from college in social work and later earned her master's degree in counseling.

Socially, Sheri was terrified of men, yet longed to be in a loving relationship. Since she was a desirable woman, she had her pick of men. She felt very uncomfortable with nice men; she inevitably rejected the ones who respected and treated her well. Her dating life consisted of spending time with emotionally unavailable men, just like her father, looking for anything to reinforce her negative feelings. Trying to win their love, as she had done continuously with her father, left her with negative results. She had several disastrous relationships with men, some of whom had various addictions. The victim mentality was firmly entrenched in her life.

When Sheri was twenty-five, she got a phone call from her mother telling her that her brother was missing. Soon it was discovered that because of money and jealousy, her stepbrother Ed had kidnapped, tortured, and buried alive her wonderful brother Sandy. Sheri was devastated. The only person that she truly loved and trusted was killed by a member of her stepfamily. She felt extremely guilty because she thought that if she had been more available, she might have been able to save her brother. To make matters worse, her mom was unable to discuss any feelings with her. Though Sheri coped as best she could, the death of Sandy, the trial of his killer, and her own emotional baggage began to take its toll on her. As a result, she developed migraine headaches. Even though she worked in mental health, she would not consider therapy because she felt she could only rely on herself.

A few years later, after many boyfriends disappointed her, she decided to take charge of her dating life. She saw Gail's ad for a relationship coach in 1990 and contacted her. Sheri initially had three sessions with Gail and then joined one of the support groups that Gail and Basha ran. In the group, Sheri started to trust others and herself.

She spent two years becoming at peace with herself and her past, not only by continuing with the group, but also by beginning individual therapy with Basha. Sheri related the following changes that occurred within herself: "When I started attending the group sessions, I was in great emotional pain. The conflicts within me, both the loss of my brother and the bizarre betrayal of my family, had taken their toll on me. As my work in the group progressed, I began to learn that I could trust all the members. They were there every week and accepted me unconditionally. I also found it therapeutic to help other group members, and in doing so, allowed myself to express my own vulnerabilities in public for the first time in my life. This was a big step for me. The group and the information I learned afforded me the opportunity to experience intimacy in a safe environment which helped me bring it into my personal life. This part of the process was critical in my emotional healing and helped me regain the trust in myself.

"With this newfound strength, I felt more confident to address family issues, especially those that I had repressed for many years. I was able to confront my parents regarding these issues and subsequently developed a stronger, more honest and authentic relationship with them. For example, because of my trust in Basha, I brought my mom into therapy to help us heal and to learn to communicate in a more direct and loving manner. This led to feeling better about myself and I began to think about what I could offer others, especially a soul mate."

As Sheri has described, her focus for the first six months, in both group and individual therapy, was working on appreciating and loving herself and healing from her past wounds—learning the Seven Spiritual Wisdoms and doing soulwork.

When Sheri felt more whole, she embarked on a new path in her social life—dating consciously—where she started implementing the soul dating skills and attitudes required to date and relate to another in an entirely new way. She immediately began to be attracted to and date nice and available men. The games that Sheri had been engaging in all her life were dropped and "Sheri's Old Book of Rules" was thrown out.

When Sheri felt ready, with Basha's encouragement, she decided to visit her dad. She knew she would never be ready for a soul mate relationship until her unfinished business was resolved. She realized that the two issues left were forgiving and healing her relationship with her father and making peace with her brother's death. She was finally able to talk to her father on a feeling level. Because of the change in her attitude, her father began to respond more positively and lovingly.

Sheri, with the encouragement of her father, took a leave of absence from work so that she could spend more quality time with him. Additionally, Sheri began to take a more active role in her physical and spiritual healing, such as seeing an acupuncturist for her headaches. This remarkable role reversal, going from victim to taking charge, had a dramatic effect on Sheri's life and attitude. Things started to fall in place for her because she finally believed she deserved to be happy. She was now ready and able to seek available, loving men who would respect and emotionally support her.

A few months later, she attended a yoga class many miles away. There, she met Neil. She knew immediately that he was different from any man she had ever encountered. He was genuine, warm, and unpretentious. They connected immediately on a soul level. She felt as though she had come home to herself when she was with him. Never before would she have been attracted to such a nice person. The depth of her work with Basha and Gail had changed her inner self and she was able to connect on a deep, intimate level with a wonderful man for the first time.

They slowly got to know each other in and out of yoga class. They discovered that they both valued intimacy and communication. Their discussions and interactions were soulful, involving shared interests, humor, vulnerabilities, affection, and sensitivities. They worked in the same field and embraced life, learning, and personal growth in a similar fashion. After a few months, things were going so well that Sheri became frightened, waiting for the hidden baggage to materialize. To her surprise, it never did! For the first time in her life, she understood what partnership meant as they became best friends. Love followed this deep friendship and slowly Neil demonstrated that he could be trusted fully. He was there for her in both the good and bad times. Sheri thought it was remarkable that, after one week of dating, he insisted on joining her in the hospital to stay with her ill father. Previous boyfriends had never been there for her, regardless of the situation.

Sheri finally began developing a loving relationship with her family. Now she was ready to give herself permission to be loved. She had learned to love and respect herself and finally was becoming a whole person seeking intimacy with a warm, caring partner. Soul mates Sheri and Neil got married the next year and are evolving *on the path toward spiritual partnership. They both believe that the strength of their relationship has grown because of the solid foundation of their friendship. This was reinforced especially during times of crisis, including the deaths of both their fathers and her stepbrother's parole hearings. Sheri attributes this transformation of her life to the work she did with Basha and Gail utilizing the Seven Spiritual Wisdoms, soulwork, and the soul dating steps.*

The journey in a soul mate relationship is filled with growth and learning. Soul mates are involved in dynamic change. The relationship changes not just once but many times. Both partners are consciously aware that emotional and spiritual growth is a driving force in their lives, both individually and as a couple. Each person needs to acknowledge that he or she is in the other's life to stretch, grow, and learn. Growth and change can be very uncomfortable, especially when you are in the process of confronting your limitations. Soul mates learn to provide a safe haven for their partners to work through their individual fears.

Soul mates are committed to each other's personal growth. They challenge each other to transcend the earthly personality limits they've set for themselves. The focus in a soul mate relationship is on evolving to become more authentic. As part of this process, each person must courageously reveal shadow issues and hold them up to the light. It takes bravery to bring them out in the open, talk about them, and find a way to overcome them. The other issues soul mates struggle with as individuals are:

◇ Remaining conscious in the process of confronting their limitations
◇ Becoming emotionally safe for the other person
◇ Healing old wounds
◇ Learning to value and develop other perspectives
◇ Putting aside their own perspective and habitual patterns to see things through their partner's eyes
◇ Continuing to surrender to higher consciousness
◇ Engaging in the process of becoming whole

Luckily, soul mates have each other to help facilitate this act of bravery. Knowing that your soul mate has been put in your life to help you achieve your life's lessons allows you to take risks that might otherwise be difficult.

The soul mate level presents challenges to people because they're making the transition from an I-based to a we-based relationship. Not only do soul mates need to work on their individual inner issues but they have to apply what they learn to the relationship as a whole. Integrating these two paths of learning and growing, both the I and the we, requires a commitment to understanding and exploring all the issues in the midst of highly intense feelings and many ups and downs. Soul mates are trying to learn how to be together as they search for the right balance. They're also struggling with giving each other enough space to grow.

In addition, soul mates attempt to align the soul and personality, which can cause confusion and power struggles—both individually and as a couple.

A soul mate relationship involves the following components:

⋄ Making a commitment to work at understanding themselves and each other emotionally and spiritually.

⋄ Speaking to each other intimately by making a commitment to revealing their thoughts, feelings, and ideas.

⋄ Enjoying being as well as doing together.

⋄ Trying to behave in an accepting and loving fashion toward one another as often as possible.

⋄ Recognizing there will be breakdowns in the process of intimacy and communication and remaining committed to work through and learn from them.

⋄ Struggling with give-and-take in the relationship.

⋄ Valuing the process of change and reinventing the relationship.

⋄ Processing the inevitable changes in needs, which could lead to power struggles.

Translating these principles into action requires a great deal of processing, communication, and dialogue about how you're going to help meet your own and each other's needs and invent the we of the relationship. Because some soul mates are beginners at this type of work, conversations will often turn into power struggles. This dialogue isn't simply confined to struggles over intellectual and physical requirements; it embraces emotional and spiritual realms.

Learning isn't limited to physical or emotional areas. Soul mates are searching for ways to transcend the physical and occupy a spiritual place; they are finding out what it means to surrender to a higher power and contribute to and learn from the universe. Soul mates recognize that they are walking on paths that have converged in order to learn lessons.

There are no guarantees soul mates will remain together forever. Typically, a breakup is precipitated because the couple can no longer learn and grow together. While soul mates may have been able to grow in the beginning of their relationship, they may find themselves unable to continue to create the we. Soul mates also break up because one person is incapable of meeting some of the other person's nonnegotiable requirements. Just because they're soul mates doesn't mean they can automatically meet each other's needs.

As challenging as a soul mate relationship is, it is also highly rewarding. It fulfills and nourishes people individually and as a couple. Soul mates feel as if they've truly come home to themselves when they're with the other person, and this is a rich and meaningful experience.

Reaching the level of soul mates is quite an accomplishment. We can manage and direct the process to find a companion or soul mate with a high probability of achieving the outcome we desire. By living the Seven Spiritual Wisdoms and doing the soulwork steps, anyone can have a meaningful and fulfilling relationship.

SPIRITUAL PARTNERSHIP

Spiritual partnership is the most spiritual and expansive type of relationship. The ability to be totally authentic and continually confront yourself is crucial if this is the relationship to which you aspire. Spiritual partners value what is real and refuse to live in illusion. They have a sense that their union is beyond the ordinary, that it transcends the normal level of consciousness; they believe that divine intervention has guided them toward each other. That divine intervention only comes when they are ready and have, from the bottom of their hearts, yearned for and asked for it. Their knowledge that the relationship represents a divine connection is so strong that they offer their future lives to God, to the contribution they're going to make to the universe, and to the service of others. To contribute to the world as a partnership—as a single, unified force—is a major goal of the relationship.

What does a spiritual partnership feel and look like? Though it has all the attributes of a soul mate relationship, it takes that union to a higher level. Imagine enjoying pure acceptance of the whole person, an acceptance that eliminates criticism and judgment from the partnership. This is the essence of unconditional love.

There is great strength in the we of a spiritual partnership. Both partners feel more complete when they are together but don't lose sight of who they are. Even when partners are doing something by themselves, they draw on the power and energy of the relationship's we. The I is elevated by the we.

There are never any power struggles in this type of relationship. Even if a disagreement occurs, it's over and resolved quickly in a win-win manner. Providing total trust and emotional safety, spiritual partners operate so much in the we that there's no need for battles over turf. Both partners have developed the ability to utilize multiple perspectives so that they can see situations, solve problems, and understand and value different points of view. Questions are always answered with the truth and there's never any holding back. Nonverbal communication is an integral part of the relationship.

Spiritual partnership is not and should not be everyone's goal; you shouldn't feel that you have failed if you achieve a companionship or soul mate relationship. You should also be aware that there are relatively few people who are spiritual partners or who have progressed from soul mates to this level. It takes an enormous amount of individual work and courage, along with divine intervention. On the other hand, the possibility of a spiritual partnership inspires us to find an element of spirituality and meaningfulness in all our relationships and to continue on our journey into the light.

SOUL DATEWORK

Before you start dating differently and learn to use the steps we discuss in part IV, you need to be honest with yourself about the type of relationship that makes sense for you. It's important to be clear about which type of relationship—companion, soul mate, or spiritual partnership—fits who you are and meets your needs for today and the future. Without this clarity, the steps in the following section will be difficult to comprehend.

As you do the following soul datework, reflect on the characteristics that define all three relationships and choose the one that feels right to you.

1. Considering all aspects of companionship, soul mate, and spiritual partner relationships, answer these questions:

◇ Who am I as a person?

◇ Which relationship supports that?

◇ What kind of we do I want?

◇ Which relationship supports both my personality and soul?

◇ Am I psychologically, emotionally, spiritually ready to find my soul mate or spiritual partner or do I desire to be in a companionship relationship?

◇ Am I willing to make the commitment and do the work to prepare for a soul mate or spiritual partner or am I comfortable in a companionship role?

2. Make a list of qualities that define who and what you are. Then ask yourself: Which relationship reasonates with me? What type of person do I see myself with? Which type of relationship reflects the kind of lifestyle I want to lead?

3. If you see yourself in a companion relationship, ask yourself as you're dating: Will I be satisfied at this level or am I willing to continue to do the work (the Seven Spiritual Wisdoms and soulwork steps) that will prepare me for a soul mate or spiritual partner? Will my companion be willing and able to grow with me to the next level?

MEDITATION

I will choose the relationship level that supports both my personality and my soul, knowing that, at any time, if I embrace the Seven Spiritual Wisdoms and do my psychospiritual work, I can move to the next level.

Soul Dating Steps

To reap the full benefits of the soul dating steps in this section, it's essential that you develop a deep understanding of the Spiritual Wisdoms, do the soulwork exercises in part I and part II, and have a good idea of the type of relationship you desire.

The soul dating steps are arranged in a specific order, each building on the preceding and contributing to the next. They are designed to have a cumulative effect, so it's best if you approach them in order.

Each soul dating step has to be internalized at your own pace. Some of the soul datework contains vital concepts relevant to soul dating and may require weeks of introspection, deliberation, and practice before you can move on to the next step. In addition, you may find you have to revisit a previous step in this section or to reflect on one or more of the Spiritual Wisdoms or the soulwork steps in part II in order to continue your progress. Issues may arise as you read a particular step that may be answered in another. In fact, as you work through these steps, you may find new answers or approaches that will help you in this process.

As you approach the soul dating steps, know that you're going to make some mistakes—you're only human. Treat yourself kindly and always maintain a sense of humor.

Soul Dating Step 1:
Soul Dating Defined

Dating is a serious process and has a different meaning and purpose for us (Basha and Gail) than it does for people who view it from a traditional perspective. In a companion relationship, the participants are not interested in connecting on a soul or intimate, emotional level. However, they can use many of our steps to help them find their appropriate partner.

16

Traditionally, most people look at dating as a means to an end. The goal is to make the dating process as short as possible, find someone they click with, and enter into a relationship. Most people go on dates with a mixture of anxiety and superficial concerns. Society encourages this approach. Think about the typical questions people ask when they hear that a friend has met someone she likes:

⬥ What does he do for a living?
⬥ Is he smart, funny, cute . . . ?
⬥ Where does he live?
⬥ What kind of car does he drive?

Traditional dating operates in a similar realm, resulting in personality-directed questions like these:

⬥ Should I kiss her goodnight?
⬥ Will my friends/family think he's successful enough?
⬥ How sexy should I dress? Is he going to find me attractive?

Soul dating, on the other hand, inspires us to look deeper and ask inner-directed questions like these:

⋄ Does he-she touch my heart and soul?
⋄ Do we share similar values?
⋄ Is he-she concerned with my well-being?
⋄ Do I feel like I've come home when I'm with him-her?

Perhaps the most significant contrast between soul dating and traditional dating involves the concept of romantic friendship. A driving force in soul dating is to seek a *romantic friendship, in which two people know, value, and accept everything (warts and all) about each other.*

Friendship is foreign to many relationships and marriages. When describing their marriages, many men and most women complain that it's easier to share important feelings with friends than with their spouses. The problem is that friendship isn't a goal of traditional dating or marriage.

With soul dating, romantic friendship is one of the goals because it starts you on the path to finding a compatible partner. Romantic friendship involves achieving true emotional intimacy—in advance of sexual intimacy. When sex occurs early in a dating relationship, lust and passion can be easily mistaken for love. In the heat of the moment, we become lost in romantic illusion.

The point of romantic friendship is knowing the whole person. Too often, we only know the romantic surface of people. We become lost in the romantic illusion of love at first sight; we focus on what we want the relationship to be rather than on what it is.

Romantic friendship involves baring the soul rather than the body; it means slowly letting the other person see you warts and all from the first date. And it means accepting who you are, who the other person is, and deciding if you want to develop a romantic friendship with the other person.

Soul dating facilitates romantic friendship by grounding people in relationship reality. That doesn't mean taking all the fun and romance out of dating. The joy and excitement of soul dating not only lasts longer (i.e., forever) but it's far more intense and deep. It's real. True friendship depends on having no secrets and letting people experience you as you really are. You don't have to like everything you learn about a soul mate. You do, however, have to accept the things you don't like and not count on anything to change.

Baring the heart, soul, and spirit rather than the body can be far more awkward and disturbing than taking off your clothes. If you haven't accepted your idiosyncrasies, history, and dysfunctions, revealing *anything* will be difficult. You need to be comfortable with who you are at the emotional and soul levels before you share these things with others.

Reaching down and bringing forth your authentic self without shame or embarrassment, starting on that first date, is the goal of beginning a romantic friendship. By sharing your authentic self, you allow intimacy to develop slowly.

The payoff is finding someone whom you connect with on all levels. It's a transcendent experience; discovering a romantic friend makes you feel like you've discovered someone you've been searching for all your life. As you begin dating in this new way, keep in mind that not every person is going to be right for you; love is not enough.

Let the following principles serve as a guide:

1. *Purpose, consciousness, and intent should guide your dating.* It should not be an arbitrary activity. By being purposeful and aware, you are proactive and in control of the dating process.

2. *Dating is a learning process.* It requires thought, discussion, and reflection.

3. *Dating is a process of discovery and a time of inquiry.* It is an opportunity to learn about yourself and another person; it is a time to find out what you value and what lifestyle meets your needs.

4. *Dating should reflect an alignment of the personality and soul.* Most people only date from their personalities.

5. *Dating is not a distinct, disconnected activity but an integral element of who you are.* It is the frosting on the cake, an addition to an already rich, satisfying life.

6. *Balance governs dating behavior.* Balance means that dating is just one element among many on the scale of one's life; it means that one

doesn't unbalance one's life to please another person ("He's a vegetarian, I'm going to become a vegetarian so he'll continue to go out with me"); needy behavior is a sign of imbalance.

7. *Dating requires time.* It takes time to learn about another person and discover if you can be together; there is no such thing as instant intimacy.

8. *Dating is fun.* It's fun to learn about yourself and another person. Because soul dating is not an all-consuming, singular activity, much of the stress and anxiety is removed from the process; it's one of many things that are important to you and can be enjoyed as part of a balanced life.

9. *Appreciate yourself and others.* Rather than try to change the people you date, understand and celebrate the differences; rather than beat yourself up for what you lack, realize what a great catch you are (or what a great catch you can be).

10. *Determine what you value as you date.* Decide what traits and behaviors meet what you want and which ones are unacceptable; date out of want and not need.

11. *Discover the who of a person, not just the what.* Take the opportunity to discover the whole person, not just external aspects of the person.

12. *Apply skills and techniques.* Take advantage of tools (such as interviewing) that help you discover who you and other people are.

13. *Overcome your fears about dating and finding a partner.* Don't date desperately and in a way that allows needy behavior to control your dating; recognize that you have something valuable to offer others and they will feel lucky to find you.

This last point is critical. We strongly believe that one reason you should date is to deal with the anxieties, insecurities, and fears you harbor regarding the dating process, understanding that these concerns are not unique to you. By dating consciously and purposefully, you'll find yourself accepting these feelings. The more you date this way, the less anxious you'll feel.

SOUL DATEWORK

The following questions can be answered in the affirmative by people who date with their personalities and souls aligned. We don't expect you to answer yes to every (or even any) question at this point in the process. What we hope is that you'll use these questions to explore who you are and why you would choose to soul date:

1. Do you date with consciousness, purpose, and intent?

2. Is your life in balance; is there a harmony between work and personal time; do you find fulfillment in family, friends, and time spent alone?

3. Are you seeking a romantic friendship; is it important to gain the acceptance, understanding, and communication that comes with a close friendship; is this something you seek when you date?

4. Are you your authentic self when you date; are you slowly revealing who you are and sharing on a soul level as well as from your personality?

5. Do you date slowly; do you take the time required to know a person— as well as yourself—before entering into a relationship?

6. Starting from the first date, do you communicate on an authentic level; do you show the other person who you really are from the first words and glances that are exchanged?

MEDITATION

I will use the process of dating as a time to get to know myself and others. I know true intimacy comes from developing a romantic friendship that will lead to my soul mate.

Soul Dating Step 2: Approachability

17

Approachable people are surrounded by an aura, a flow of energy. Even when they're silent, people gravitate toward them. They're completely comfortable with themselves; their ease with who they are allows their authentic self to shine through.

Approachability isn't a superficial concept. It's far more than just being friendly and open. From a soul dating perspective, it consists of the signals we send out into the world that are picked up by receptive others. When you are approachable, every movement you make and every word you speak resonate with your heart and soul. You mirror on the outside what's going on inside. The more you slowly reveal of yourself, the more likely you are to attract people on your wavelength. Energy attracts like energy.

As a soul dater, approachability isn't about attracting more people, but attracting the right people. You can't do this if you don't know who you are and haven't embraced your shadow.

Approachability reveals itself in the language we use in getting to know others, and we all express ourselves differently. One person's approachable style may be direct and assertive, while another person's style may be reflective and quiet. Flirting, for instance, is a perfectly acceptable form of approachability if it reflects who you really are. If it conceals who you are, however, flirting will attract the wrong people.

The concept of approachability also has a broader meaning. It evolves throughout the beginning of the relationship as you get to know the person better. As you become more comfortable and secure in the relationship, you will naturally spend more time together. Consequently, you will become more vulnerable and your deeper level of approachability expands.

While personal styles are different, approachability is a highly intentional and conscious process. As part of that process, you need to be aware of several things:

⋄ How you think and feel about yourself
⋄ How you use body language—verbal and nonverbal:
  —How you speak and what you say
  —How you use gestures, expressions, and personal space
⋄ How you dress, wear your hair, and use jewelry and other symbols of self

You need to be aware of these things so that you don't sabotage yourself. When the personality and the soul aren't aligned, we send the wrong message: we dress in a sexy, provocative manner and attract the wrong type of people. We haven't done our inner work, and so our external self doesn't reflect who we really are.

We often use external elements to disguise rather than reveal who we are. Consciously or unconsciously, we wear our hair a certain way or favor a certain style of speech that masks our real self. Afraid or unable to reveal every aspect of our persona, we create a misleading approachability. We attract people who will never become our romantic friends or soul mates.

Truly approachable individuals project an aura; it's as if their souls are shimmering. When your personality and soul are in alignment, you naturally project this aura. Others who have done their inner work will naturally resonate to that aura. They can feel the energy you're throwing off, and in their souls they sense that it matches their own.

To help yourself achieve this approachable state, you need to do the following:

⋄ Communicate that you feel good about yourself, you're at ease with all parts of yourself, and you're not afraid of others.

⋄ Come from an inner place of genuineness that reflects warmth, caring, and openness.

⋄ Reduce other people's fear of being rejected; the more approachable you are, the less afraid others are of your rejecting them.

⋄ Learn to share your feelings with safe people; whether you're sad or glad, irritable or excited, let them see the whole you.

⋄ Let appropriate people closer to you so they can get to know you; be selective about your inner circle and whom you date.

Given the benefits of being approachable, you would think that people would naturally attempt to achieve this state. In fact, many successful businesspeople—especially those in sales—are terrific at being approachable in work situations because they are only sharing the what of who they are in a doing activity. Yet these same people have great difficulty at achieving the same state in their personal lives. The dilemma is that dating requires much deeper levels of approachability because this process reflects who we are rather than what we are. Unlike most work interactions, soul dating demands that we reveal authentic parts of the self. The fear many of us have is that if we expose these vulnerable layers, others will find us unlikable or unlovable.

Many of us come from dysfunctional families, who put us down for being ourselves. We were taught to conceal. The lesson of approachability, as you've learned from the Spiritual Wisdoms and soulwork steps, is that we need to heal these old wounds and reveal who we really are.

When we first met Natalie, we were struck with how attractive, poised, and self-confident she appeared. As we were to learn, she was the vice president of a major corporation, had impeccable taste in clothes, and maintained a close circle of intimate friends. Surprisingly, she felt unsuccessful in the dating arena. She was divorced twice and, because of past family messages, maintained feelings of shame concerning her two "failures." Though she dated, she didn't attract the type of men she wanted; she revealed at the first class how discouraged she felt, having no direction or hope. Over the years, Natalie had completed a great deal of inner soul searching, met regularly with a therapist, read spiritual books, and attended numerous work-

shops. She had a rich spiritual life, talking daily with, as she said, "my best friend— God."

As we started discussing what it meant to be approachable, she quietly listened, later asking for direct feedback. As we talked, it became apparent that her shame and embarrassment revealed themselves in her outward manner appearing to be withholding, aloof, and somewhat cold—an impression contrary to what she wanted to give. As the weeks passed, Natalie came to realize and accept that her divorces taught her life lessons. She accepted that there wasn't anything inherently wrong with her and that being human is to make mistakes. Becoming more accepting of who she was, she consciously shifted her attitude and started mirroring on the outside what she felt on the inside. By making eye contact, smiling easily, initiating small talk, and revealing her innermost authentic self, men were drawn toward her like magnets. As she announced at the last class session, "I'm dating men I really like, who really like me. Men are great!"

It's useful to familiarize yourself with some of the traits of approachable people. While people develop different styles of approachability, certain traits transcend these styles. These traits facilitate openness, honesty, and self-expression—not just in you, but in those you meet:

◇ *Stay focused and centered on the person.* Do not allow your attention to wander; learn to live in the moment, and if your attention should wander, apologize and refocus.

◇ *Ask open-ended questions* that can't be answered with just a yes or no; these questions require people to dig deeper for their answers.

◇ *Maintain an open body stance.* Direct eye contact, smiling, and other aspects of your body language communicate receptivity to being approached.

◇ *Share low-vulnerable information.* Expose a feeling or anything that carries a mild emotional charge for you—for example, "This is the first time I've gone to a party without a date and I'm nervous." This low-vulnerable statement reveals an authentic aspect of who you are. Pay attention to how the other person responds.

◇ *Establish a dialogue rather than a monologue* in opening small talk. Demonstrate that you're interested, not just interesting; ask the other person questions; attempt to establish a flow of words that is natural and energizing.

◇ *Develop a look that mirrors the inner you.* Strive to make your clothing, hair, jewelry, and other outer symbols correspond to who you really are; attract the kind of people you want to attract.

SOUL DATEWORK

First impressions count when it comes to approachability. Your initial presentation, attitude, and enthusiasm determine whom you attract. To improve your ability to reflect your most authentic self, do the following:

1. You only have five minutes to communicate who you are to another person. Pretend you're answering an ad or have just met someone at a party and you need to capture your essence in five minutes. What would you share about yourself? Write down your answer.

2. When you meet someone, tell that person something personal and meaningful to your life that happened recently. Pay attention to how the other person responds. Is she empathetic or dismissive? Does he offer something meaningful and personal about his own life?

3. *Approachability is a natural process with no goal other than self-expression and openness. It is the way of expressing the inner you using outward behaviors.* Given our definition of approachability, think of someone you know who fits that definition. Write ten words that describe this individual's approachable style.

4. Now write a paragraph describing the messages that person sends you based on his or her approachable style. Use the list of approachability traits beginning on p. 111 to help you with your description.

5. Share our definition of approachability with a few friends who will give you honest feedback. Do they see you as you would like to be seen?

What are you doing that pushes people away rather than attracting the right type of person?

6. Choose an approachability trait you would like to perfect or learn and begin practicing it, first on friends and then on dates. Don't choose a behavior that you admire in others if it seems unnatural or wrong for you. You want to find a trait that you value and now are allowing to emerge. It may be anything from an authentic smile to sharing a vulnerability.

This is a *stretching* exercise and might not feel comfortable at first. By *stretching*, we mean going beyond your comfort zone and the limits you've set for yourself. You bring parts of yourself to the surface that you haven't allowed to emerge before, and this may be a struggle at first. If so, don't try for a big step. Choose something small and easy to bring forth, and then add something a bit more significant.

7. Complete this sentence: *"I am afraid to be approachable because* _____ [I'm unattractive; I'll have nothing to say; I'll be rejected; etc.]."

Whatever you filled in the blank with, it needs to be made conscious, acknowledged, and worked through. Once that's done, you'll find the *stretching* exercise much easier to do.

MEDITATION

I am open to being approachable to others and recognize when others are being approachable to me. I will send a clear signal of who I am and be more selective and receptive to the signals of others.

Soul Dating Step 3: Romantic Illusion

18

Romantic illusion is seductive, luring us with its promise of perfect love and head-over-heels romance. The notion of love at first sight is enormously appealing, and it's not hard to see why our society is addicted to romantic illusion.

We're hooked on an illusion manufactured by love songs, romance novels, and other forms of popular culture, and it leads us to form relationships with the wrong people. Under romantic illusion's spell, we may believe we've found the ideal person and that the relationship will last forever. But time and experience show this belief to be an illusion, and a cruel one at that. No one can live up to it.

As the phrase implies, romantic illusion involves misperceptions about love. Here are some common ways we misperceive:

⬥ Falling in love with someone's possibilities rather than seeing who they really are; fantasizing about who they will become or who you want them to be.

⬥ Believing in love at first sight.

⬥ Being convinced that we have found the missing parts of ourself in another person and now we are whole.

⬥ Feeling that love should be elusive, mysterious, and hot.

⬥ Ecstatically adoring another person who appears to be absolutely perfect.

⬧ Experiencing a powerful, purely sexual response to another individual that overwhelms everything else.

⬧ Getting caught up in the externals of love—beauty, money, sex—and ignoring the inner dimensions.

Romantic illusion deceives us, making us think we've found a permanent soul mate when what we've really found is a temporary lover. Certainly pop culture has created a fertile environment for romantic illusion to blossom. It focuses our attention on externals, and we mistake passion and lust for love. When we meet someone who fulfills the fantasies engendered by romance novels or movies, we sigh, "He looks just like Brad Pitt," and we're goners.

George, a divorced CPA in the throes of romantic illusion, reported he had been out six times with Joan and knew he had found the woman of his dreams. She was attractive, bright, and had her own apartment, and the sex was great. He kept saying over and over, "I can't find anything wrong with her."

What's so wrong with that? What's so wrong with mistaking passion and lust for love? What's wrong is that it's not grounded in anything real, and it's why people wake up one day after they've been in a relationship and ask themselves, "Who is this stranger?"

When we fall victim to romantic illusion, four negative things happen:

1. *We look for a perfect person when there's no such thing as perfection.* No one can live up to our ideal lover; we search for the high of intense passion rather than accepting the natural ebb and flow of love.

2. *We stay in bad relationships because we're caught up in the fantasy of what we want it to be.* In turn, we give up so much to be in the relationship that we feel empty inside, and we cling to our partners because they seem to be all we have.

3. *We focus on people who immediately turn us on.* We arouse our passion and lust rather than build a romantic friendship where love grows better the more you get to know the other person.

Miranda put an ad in the personals. One evening she spoke with Carlos for hours and was extremely excited about meeting him. He seemed to have all the right credentials—late thirties, never married, employed, and funny. She was sure he was going to be "the one." The next night at class, we were anxious to hear how her date went. "Oh, I didn't like him. There was no chemistry." Simon, a class member, asked, "What was wrong with him? Didn't he treat you right?"

"No, he was a perfect gentleman," Miranda replied, "refined and cute. We had some things in common but it's what I said, I'm just not interested—no instant chemistry!"

Miranda is looking for someone to engage her hormones, not her soul or heart.

4. *We maintain romantic illusion for a long time, well into dating and even marriage.* We remain unconscious, allowing the illusion to cloud our true goals and values.

You need to be open to another type of attraction than the one romantic illusion encourages. When you connect with a soul partner:

◇ You mutually share authentic issues and concerns that establish the inner connection.

◇ You are unusually comfortable with the other person; there's a warm, affectionate quality to the relationship and you feel as if you've come home.

◇ You feel a sense of déjà vu in which a strong connection exists between you; it's as if you've always known this person.

◇ You feel better about yourself in the presence of this person; there's a meeting of heart, spirit, and mind.

By getting past romantic illusion, you give soulful love a chance to happen and avoid the bitter disappointment and hurt that often comes with the conventional dating process.

Dispelling romantic illusion isn't easy. It's a powerful drug; it puts people in a temporary (very temporary) state of euphoria, and society is addicted to it. To break the habit, you first have to act against your feelings, break old patterns, and do what seems unnatural and impossible.

The soul dating process, however, is very effective at helping people move past romantic illusion.

SOUL DATEWORK

1. People suffering from romantic illusion commonly make or think the following statements. Place a check mark next to the ones that you identify with:

◇ When I meet my perfect partner, I will be transformed.
◇ My partner will never leave me and I will be safe forever.
◇ Love at first sight means real love.
◇ The ideal relationship will never change.
◇ This perfect relationship will fix me and make life easy.
◇ I have no need to learn about love or consciously develop the skills of love.
◇ There will be no disagreement between me and my partner.
◇ Having a relationship is infinitely better than having no relationship.
◇ I'll make my true love fall in love with me.
◇ I'll be anything my partner wants me to be.
◇ Love is all I need.
◇ If there's no instant chemistry, there's no chance of love.

2. Place a check next to the following "romantic illusion" words you've used to describe someone you've dated:

◇ Swept away
◇ Love at first sight
◇ Spontaneous combustion
◇ Lust
◇ My perfect partner
◇ Dream lover
◇ My fantasy
◇ Instant chemistry

3. Reflect on how romantic illusion has made it difficult for you to develop a soulful relationship.

MEDITATION

I see how romantic illusion has moved me away from the possibility of a soulful partnership; I will now date with realistic expectations and search for an emotional and spiritual connection that will lead to a romantic friendship.

Soul Dating Step 4: Emotional Safety

Emotional safety is something you need to strive for in yourself and look for in another person. Specifically, individuals who love themselves and work at becoming whole have reached a point where emotional safety is becoming a natural part of who they are. It's a two-way street of openness, vulnerability, and acceptance reflected in a combination of words, body language, and attitudes.

19

Meeting the criteria for being an emotionally safe person can be defined by the following traits:

- ◇ Respecting limits and boundaries
- ◇ Telling the truth consistently and compassionately
- ◇ Not becoming enmeshed or codependent
- ◇ Not using anything you reveal—information, fears, or vulnerabilities—against you
- ◇ Feeling you can be open and not have to protect yourself
- ◇ Not being judgmental and blaming
- ◇ Sharing fears, insecurities, flaws, and weaknesses

When soul dating, it's important to understand what another person's attitudes, words, and actions say about his ability to be emotionally safe. One of the ways to do this is by setting limits and boundaries and observing whether the other person honors them. These boundaries (or limits) can be anything you feel strongly about, from music you dislike to behaviors you find offensive. From the first date on, you should start setting boundaries. For instance, you might share a low vulnerable such as your unwillingness to sit in the smoking section of a restaurant. If your date says, "Oh, you'll get used to it, just give it a try," he clearly has ignored the boundary you've established, which indicates he is not an emotionally safe person for you.

There are times when you'll need to say to the person you're dating, "This behavior is fine, but this other behavior is not." This boundary-setting may require you to meet your own needs at times rather than meeting the needs of someone else. It may even require you to leave, to get away from this person and be by yourself for a while. An emotionally safe individual will understand and accept the boundaries that you establish.

Emotionally safe people try telling the truth consistently and compassionately. Rather than accusing you of doing something wrong, judging you to be bad or dumb because of it, they work on offering you caring advice. When dating, be alert to whether someone is able to tell you something about yourself in a caring and helpful way.

Certain people have difficulty with emotional safety because they come from emotionally unsafe backgrounds. For instance, if you were abused as a child, you'll find it very difficult (without a significant amount of inner work) to achieve the trust and intimacy that are essential for emotional safety. Or you may have had parents who modeled unsafe attitudes or behaviors. For instance, you may have had highly critical parents who were always blaming and never were satisfied with what you did. As an adult, you may find yourself trying to please the people you go out with in the same way you tried and failed to please your parents. Gail describes her enmeshed, codependent family dynamic this way:

I grew up in an environment where few emotional boundaries were honored. Everyone knew everyone else's business and what I felt and did was closely monitored by a family who never were quite satisfied.

Everyone was always in my face, and when I had moments of rebellion and tried to express my individuality, all hell would break loose. Cajoling, arguing, yelling, silence were all used to sway me back to the fold. It always worked. As a young woman in my twenties, I was not able to pick out clothes without the approval of the group. I never felt safe or appreciated for being just me, knowing I always had to adapt to the family way.

When I did get married, everyone approved. But even on our honeymoon, I remember feeling very disconnected from my husband, like something was missing, and when we did have decisions to make as a couple, I checked first with the family before I gave him my opinion. I never had confidence in his viewpoints (even though he was bright and a good decision maker) unless I first conferred with the clan.

Looking back, of course I realize how detrimental this way of operating was to the marriage. How could my husband feel secure and count on me to be in his corner? It's no wonder we got divorced. Only then did I go into therapy and begin to break away from this enmeshed family dynamic. When my mother died, she was clearly upset with me for breaking the unhealthy emotional connection I had with my family. She never understood why I needed to.

Over twenty years ago, I made a conscious decision to never again be in a situation where my boundaries weren't separate and distinct, both emotionally and physically, from family, friends, lovers. Therefore, even though Ed and I have been in a committed relationship for many years, I have deliberately chosen not to get married or live with him. (I'm pretty sure this would be with any man I'd be with.) This is the only way I can make sure that no one will tell me how to live or what to do. This is my way of taking care of myself and feeling safe.

As you are assessing your relationship for emotional safety, you should also be alert for power struggles. When you find yourself engaged in a battle over emotional turf, you've entered unsafe territory. As soon as you hear things like "We always do what you want to do" or "This time we're going where I want to go," then you're hearing unsafe words, signaling the time to have a serious discussion about your personal boundaries.

Developing emotional safety is impossible if we can't separate our own feelings and opinions from someone else's. Enmeshment and codependency are two common ways of describing this situation. The following questions will help you determine what events in the past may have damaged your ability to form emotionally safe relationships:

⬥ Did anyone refuse to respect your private time or privacy?

⬥ Was there a relationship in which you felt you had merged with the other person and lost your individuality?

⬥ Did someone in your family presume to know how you thought and felt?

◇ Growing up, was your family unit considered more important than each person's individual identity?

◇ When you became older and began to separate yourself from your family, did they continue to try to tell you how to live your life, acting judgmental and critical?

◇ Did you come from a family where no one gave you feedback or they told you that everything you did was bad (or that everything you did was good)?

The following describes behaviors of people who are lost or merged with another person:

◇ They ignore their own feelings while experiencing someone else's feelings very intensely.

◇ They pretend that their opinions and interests are the same as their date's, lover's, or spouse's.

◇ They become sexually involved with someone before they are ready, in order to establish or maintain a relationship.

◇ They accept another person's point of view while discounting their own.

◇ They change their plans at the last minute to suit the whim of their date or partner.

◇ They are in a state of constant giving—of time, talents, money, services, and so on.

SOUL DATEWORK

1. To restore your emotional safety, try these exercises:

◇ State your preferences daily; create a list of things you prefer to do (e.g., going to one restaurant versus another).

◇ Create a list of limits and share them with others (e.g., "I am willing to go camping with you once a year, but I am not willing to spend three weeks in the wilderness with you and your camping buddies.").

◇ Be aware of what limits you're comfortable setting and which ones give you trouble.

◇ Practice disagreeing and feeling comfortable with it. Acknowledge the other person's opinion and then restate your own.

2. To determine the emotional safety of others:

◇ Start out by creating a list of behaviors (both words and actions) a date might do to indicate he's emotionally safe, such as:

◇ *John actively listened to Mary and while he did not agree with her opinion, John didn't criticize her or make her wrong for having a different point of view.*

◇ *Sally shared with Tom her fear of speaking in front of her sales staff. Tom empathized and, in turn, expressed his trepidations when speaking in public, something he did on a regular basis.*

◇ Create another list of behaviors (both words and actions) a date might do to indicate he's emotionally unsafe, such as:

◇ *Diane shared with Don the recurring concern she had about her occasional shortness and impatience with her friends and family. At the time, Don seemed empathetic, but weeks later, in a moment of frustration, he yelled at Diane, "You're always abrupt with me. Of course, what can I expect, you're that way with everybody else, too."*

◇ *Sam and Tish had an intimate, caring friendship. Yet every time there was dissention between them, Sam threatened to leave the relationship.*

3. Are you an emotionally safe person for someone else? Refer back to the list on page 119 to see if you're meeting the criteria.

MEDITATION

I only allow people in my life who are emotionally safe, honor my feelings, and accept my individuality. I also am continuously working at being emotionally safe for others.

Soul Dating Step 5:
Self-Talk

20

Becoming aware of the conversations we have with our-selves is a key step on the soul dating path. Self-talk goes on all the time, and can be both positive and negative. Knowing what we believe, as reflected in our self-talk, affects how we feel and behave. The goal is to listen, learn, and grow from it.

Many people use self-talk masochistically. They berate themselves for not being smart enough, pretty enough, or sociable enough. Conscious people approach their self-talk with a hunger for the truth; they listen to both the positive and the negative conversations and learn from what they hear. They know the goal is not to judge themselves; it's simply to listen impartially, ask for evidence, and grow.

The *first principle* in examining self-talk is to know that negative self-talk is usually not true and can sabotage us. Most of us have come back from a date or a party and berated ourselves, saying:

- ⬥ "I'm too shy."
- ⬥ "I'm unattractive."
- ⬥ "I'm boring."
- ⬥ "I talk too much."
- ⬥ "I'm not smart enough."

By exaggerating our flaws and faults, we lose touch with who we really are. Removed from the personal truth of our behavior, we have difficulty dating and establishing romantic friendships because we believe this false information. In turn, we behave differently, which pushes people away. Negative self-talk can become so destructive that it keeps people im-mobilized and afraid to date.

What we need to do is ground the information to find out what the truth really is. To ground self-talk simply means to be conscious of what you are saying and to ask for evidence. This process helps you become a nonjudgmental observer.

When we work with someone to get to the truth of the self-talk, we find it useful to employ a question-and-answer process. For example, if someone is beating herself up by saying, "I'm unattractive," we would ask, *"Why do you say that?"*

"Because I have a big nose."

"How do you know this makes you unattractive to everyone?"

"Because a guy told me I was unattractive."

"So you decided this was true because one guy told you?"

"Another guy said the same thing."

"So you've given these two people the power to make you unattractive?"

This questioning process brings us back to reality. The woman who is twenty pounds overweight tells herself that she's so heavy that no one will ever marry her.

"Does that mean no one has ever found you attractive?"

"Well, no, but they don't find me as attractive as others."

"Well, that may be, but some men have found you desirable and attractive. Therefore, women who are twenty pounds overweight (you) can find a partner."

Grounding ourselves in the truth puts flaws in perspective. We come to accept that our big nose or shyness is just a part of who we are. Sometimes, this questioning leads us to discover the real truth. It may be so that we have a large nose, but that's not what's turning guys off; it's the fact that we're unable to make eye contact or are too needy.

When we determine the truth of our self-talk, we have choices. By making peace with being twenty pounds overweight, we must accept the fact that society considers it less desirable. Consequently, there will be fewer men available to date. Our other choice, however, is to embrace this societal belief, decide to lose the weight, and create a new reality. Either way, this eliminates the anger and resentment we feel.

On the other hand, it's possible that our negative self-talk is the truth. For example, we tell ourselves, "I monopolize too much of the conversation, maybe that's why I'm not successful at dating." After hearing this, we need to observe our behavior with others to assess if, indeed, this may be true. Seeing the truth forces us to develop the skills necessary to achieve the desired result.

The *second principle* in examining self-talk is to know that positive self-talk also may not be true. For example, Lydia might tell herself what a great listener she is. She's proud of her ability to listen quietly as others talk about themselves, and she really thinks that this ability is considered an attribute by men she dates. In reality, this positive self-talk is inaccurate, and it sabotages Lydia. While it's true that she sits quietly while others talk, her attention wanders easily and she doesn't remember much of what others tell her. In fact, her stone-faced, unresponsive quality has ended more than one promising relationship prematurely. Considering Lydia's story, if we accept everything we say to ourselves as the truth, and we don't ground our self-talk based on what most people believe to be true, we can sabotage the results we hope to achieve.

To be effective as a soul dater, we need to pay attention to our inner dialogues in order to learn the truth about how we might be subverting the dating process.

SOUL DATEWORK

Sometimes we let our self-talk run on and on without paying attention. The first step is to listen to what we say to ourselves.

1. Verbalize and write out your self-talk before or after an important social situation. Listen to yourself when you come home from a party or after you've met someone to whom you're attracted. Pay attention to what inner dialogue is taking place.

2. Search for the truth in your self-talk. The following questions might help you ground it. Remember, to ground self-talk means to be conscious of what you are telling yourself and to ask for evidence.

◇ How do you know that your self-talk is true?
◇ What recent social situations have you been in that support or disprove the self-talk statement?
◇ Are you basing your self-talk on only one or two negative experiences?

3. Once you've determined the truth of your self-talk statements, ask yourself if you want to change to get the results you desire. If so, what changes would you make?

MEDITATION

I will listen to my positive and negative self-talk without judgment. I will ground this self-talk in the truth and use what I learn to grow and date consciously.

Soul Dating Step 6:
Needy Dating Behavior

Singles who are codependent or needy have a difficult time dating. They immediately jump into a relationship or stay too long in an unhealthy situation because they haven't learned to rely on themselves for inner strength and emotional stability. Because they feel empty, they depend on others to fill them up. A needy person has an insatiable appetite and those around them always feel drained. It's impossible for needy people to attract a soul mate, someone with a full, rich inner and outer life, because they haven't learned to live some of the Wisdoms.

21

Let's take the case of Leticia. She came to class bursting to tell us of an experience she'd recently had with a "great-looking needy guy." On her first date with Jerome, he brought her flowers and took her to a very expensive restaurant. As the evening wore on, he continuously complimented her on her good looks, humor, and intelligence, and subtly suggested that he thought she was the woman of his dreams. Leticia felt uncomfortable, but admonished herself for not being able to accept compliments. At the end of the evening, he asked her out again and she said yes, because, after all, he was handsome, an administrator of a large healthcare facility, and she didn't want to hurt his feelings.

The next day, a dozen red roses were delivered to her office and Jerome called three times to tell her what a terrific, adorable woman she is. Over the next week, Leticia suggested he go more slowly but he ignored her, only to bombard her with more flowers, calls, cards, and expensive gifts.

Leticia continued, "In the past, because I wasn't feeling comfortable with all this, I would have thought there was something wrong with me. After all, he was giving me the attention I dreamed about. But now, all I felt was smothered by someone who doesn't even know me. It was a relief to tell him I didn't want to see him again, even though for days he tried to convince me I was making a terrible mistake."

Needy dating behaviors take many forms. Let's start with a list of characteristic actions:

⬧ Coming on too strong (e.g., calling three times a day after the first date)
⬧ Bombarding someone with gifts, flowers, candy, or cards
⬧ Attempting to manipulate another person into liking them via nonstop talking or complimenting
⬧ Acting crazy about someone without really knowing the person
⬧ Falling in love at a moment's notice
⬧ Dating someone (anyone) just to have a date
⬧ Rushing into sex
⬧ Revealing too much information too fast without determining if the other person is emotionally safe
⬧ Putting life on hold until a relationship is established (e.g., not taking trips, buying a condo, or establishing a financial portfolio)

Neediness or codependency makes you not only act but feel certain ways. See if your feelings mirror the following needy traits:

⬧ Your ups and downs are determined by how other people treat you.
⬧ You don't know how to spend time with yourself.
⬧ You feel empty inside.
⬧ You give only with conditions.
⬧ You have difficulty hearing and saying no.
⬧ You only feel okay when you're dating or in a relationship.
⬧ You imagine marriage right after meeting someone.
⬧ You feel panic if you're not dating or in a relationship.

Here's a third way needy behavior manifests itself. Certain expressions and negative self-talk crop up in the conversations of needy people. Here are some of the telling phrases they may say to themselves:

⬥ "I feel sorry for myself."
⬥ "I have an empty place inside of me that needs to be filled up by someone."
⬥ "The only way I'm going to have a life is through another person."
⬥ "My moods and behavior are directly related to how someone treats me."
⬥ "I feel compelled to go out even though I really want to stay home."
⬥ "I'm afraid (or don't like) to be alone."
⬥ "Maybe this is the best I can hope for."
⬥ "I don't deserve any better."

People who exhibit needy behaviors, feelings, and talk are human "do-ers", not human "be-ings". Soul daters, in contrast, have learned to incorporate being moments and activities into their lives. They've found that when they do, their dating desperation and neediness gradually disappear.

Sandy was the CEO of a Fortune 500 company, owned a lakeside condo, and drove a BMW. Yet she repeatedly told us how lonely, sad, and empty she felt and how desperately she wanted to be in love. She had never been without a man, drifting from one unfulfilling relationship to another. Whenever she stayed home in her lavish apartment, she either spent her time on the phone, wrote letters to out-of-state relatives, or sat by the computer editing work-related material.

We suggested she stop going outside of herself to fill up her emptiness, by giving up the phone calls and busy work that kept her from having moments of being with herself. We also suggested she stop dating. She looked at us incredulously, but, because she felt so hopeless, she took a leap of faith.

Months later she reported her life had shifted drastically. "At first I thought I'd never be able to do it, but gradually I started to rely on myself and my inner connection to the universe. Now if I don't get my daily dose of 'me,' I start to feel out of sorts. I also don't feel like I need to be with a man. Don't get me wrong, I want a man, but one that will embellish my life, not someone that fills in the vacuum."

This state of wholeness is actually something that just about anyone can achieve by becoming intimately involved in the Spiritual Wisdoms and soulwork. Following is a short review of some of the important points from the Spiritual Wisdoms to consider:

◇ Face your truths without judgment or blame.
◇ Get clarity on what you value by using your heart, intuition, and feelings.
◇ Learn to live in the moment, with no expectations of tomorrow.
◇ Remember what is important and meaningful in life.
◇ Acknowledge your spiritual and emotional needs.
◇ Celebrate your strengths by having compassion for, accepting, and loving yourself.
◇ Heal old psychological and emotional wounds and embrace your fears.
◇ Lead a balanced life.

SOUL DATEWORK

1. *Determine your particular brand of needy behavior.* Make a list of the different ways you exhibit needy behavior (use the lists found earlier in this chapter and add your own).

2. *Visualize yourself as the water in a pitcher.* Every day you pour out a little of yourself to work, exercise, chores, family, and friends. Ask yourself, "How do I replenish the water?"

3. *List ways you can spend time on being, so you can nurture and heal yourself.* Remember, being activities are things you can experience yourself that foster introspection and contemplation and help you get in touch with your higher self. Use the list below or add your own ways of being. Start today, and resolve to spend thirty minutes each day replenishing yourself.

Taking a bubble bath
Reading (not work-related materials)
Walking (in the woods, on the beach, etc.)
Going to the zoo
Journaling
Horseback riding
Drinking coffee on the patio
Going to the library

Visiting a museum
Writing poetry
Playing a musical instrument
Playing with your pet
Watching a sunrise or sunset
Practicing yoga
Meditating

4. *Stop dating.* This allows you to spend more time being and less time doing. No matter who asks you out or whom you want to ask out, resist the impulse. Give yourself a dateless period of time, no less than two months. Voluntarily going dateless is very different from doing so involuntarily. In the latter instance, you may feel lonely and depressed. But when you stop dating intentionally, you are in control. You are driven by a purpose. Though this step is difficult at first, it will ultimately be liberating. It frees you to be yourself, so that when you resume dating you'll have eliminated the needy behaviors of the past.

5. *Remember why you dated.* To make stopping dating easier, keep in mind the needy behaviors and social pressures that might have driven you to date:

◇ Loneliness
◇ Not wanting people to think you were antisocial or strange
◇ Someone asked you
◇ Your friends or family said you'd be crazy not to go out with him or her
◇ You hadn't been on a date for weeks and worried that something was wrong with you
◇ Concern that if you didn't keep dating, you would never find someone to marry
◇ You were missing sex or physical intimacy
◇ Being a couple is more socially acceptable than being single
◇ Dating validates your desirability
◇ Dating kept you from facing other issues (a dysfunctional family history, a fear of being alone, etc.)

6. *Go back to chapter 16*, "Soul Dating Defined," and review the positive reasons for dating.

7. *Reflect.* During this dateless period, go back and review the Spiritual Wisdoms and soulwork.

MEDITATION

I have the courage to acknowledge my needy behavior. I am willing and open to take a break from dating. I look forward to this peaceful alternative as a time for reassessment and renewal. I honor my ability to rely on my inner resources to fill me up.

Soul Dating Step 7:
Dateable or Mateable

Are you dateable or mateable? Before answering, consider that it's terribly easy to fool yourself about your relationship status. It's also easy to be fooled by others. We assume we're mateable because we want to get married or we assume others are dateable because they seem casual and carefree. Dateable and mateable are not always visible attributes. It takes a certain amount of questioning to determine if we (or others) are dateable or mateable.

22

The goal of this step is to help you make that determination and assist those of you who are interested in making the transition from dateable to mateable. We want to emphasize up front that we're not making value judgments about mateable versus dateable. We're not telling you that mateable is a state everyone should aspire to. Some people are at a point in their life where they prefer to be dateable.

DATEABLE

We've identified three basic types of dateable people. Your ability to recognize these types will be valuable by helping you to decipher if the person you're first meeting or seeing suits your own standards.

Type I: Mr. or Ms. Fun and Excitement

The first type is focused on the externals—looks, money, and other personality issues. Most Type I people bounce from one relationship to the next and are waist-deep in romantic illusion, lust, and chemistry. If you were to ask them what they would want from another person, they would list superficial traits. Image is everything to them, and they're into superficial conversations and activities. They have an adolescent preoccupation with date excitement, an unwillingness to make long-term commitments, and a lack of responsibility in certain areas (career, sex, etc.).

At the same time, however, these people make great dates. They know how to have fun and create dating excitement; some of them are Don Juans (or Doña Juanas) and love the chase. This type of person values his freedom above all else. The fact that they're so much fun can cause misperceptions about who they are. When we get caught up in the dating heat they generate, we assume that they're mateable; however, a great date does not necessarily make a great mate. With this type, we can mistake lust for love and dateable for mateable.

Brad is a good example of a Type I dateable. Brad had just joined one of our groups when he announced that he had met a gorgeous, amazing woman who drives a Porsche and lives in a luxurious condo. "After three weeks of going out with her and having nothing but fun and lots of great sex, I can't find a single thing wrong," he told the group.

Brad and his "amazing woman" are both Type I dateable people. Brad is Type I because he's deep into romantic illusion and lust but also because he's with a woman who's also just into fun and sex.

Type II: Mr. or Ms. Too Good to Be True

This second type of dateable individual talks the mateable talk but doesn't follow through. It's very easy to mistake this dateable person for mateable because he shares vulnerabilities, works on personal growth, values spirituality and community service, and says he's ready to commit when he finds the right person. He is a great friend and demonstrates a capacity for emotional intimacy with his parents and children. If you just listen to what he says, you'll be convinced he's mateable.

Bob was a Type II dateable person, though he sounded to Joyce like one of the most mateable guys she had ever met. They met each other at a spiritual retreat and started going out when they returned to the city. Over the next few months, they spent a lot of time together and shared sensitive and emotional issues. Both of them practiced yoga and meditated daily. Though Bob had gone through a relatively recent divorce that involved three kids, he claimed he was almost ready for a commitment if he found the right person.

As connected as they were, emotionally and spiritually, Bob seemed to remain emotionally attached to his ex-wife and children. Joyce also felt as if she were begging Bob to spend more time with her and intuitively believed he had difficulty bonding. While he continued to insist that he loved her and wanted to be in a committed relationship, the closer Joyce tried to get, the more he pulled away.

There is no doubt that Bob had some mateable characteristics, but he was also withholding and had trouble making a deep commitment. Bob and Joyce were soul mates, but as long as Bob avoided doing his psychological work, he could never be in a mateable partnership.

Type III: Mr. or Ms. Needy

The way to identify this dateable Type III person is to observe his or her behavior, attitude, and values. Type III people desperately need a relationship but for the wrong reasons. These people reveal their dateable status when they exhibit some of the following unhealthy, needy traits:

⋄ Demonstrating some needy dating behavior
⋄ Acting secretive or revealing too much
⋄ Being unable to respect limits or hear no
⋄ Refusing to see you for who you really are, substituting their own fantasy
⋄ Having a controlling personality
⋄ Being highly critical
⋄ Losing themselves in other people
⋄ Believing relationships will change or fix their lives
⋄ Not working on aligning soul and personality
⋄ Failing to live soulful values or address past history/wounds
⋄ Possessing addictive behaviors

FROM DATEABLE TO MATEABLE

In addition, there are some people who are dateable but don't fit one of these three types. They may have just ended a long-term relationship and need time to heal or they may need to focus on personal growth and learning, including what they want in a relationship. They may be inexperienced daters or haven't dated for years and may want to date a variety of people and just have fun. The important thing to remember is not to delude yourself or others into thinking you're mateable when you're really dateable. Remember, having *some* dateable qualities still qualifies you as dateable. Most people have a mixture of dateable and mateable traits and find themselves at different points on the dateable to mateable continuum. Where are you on this continuum?

•Dateable   >   >   >   Mateable•

Although many people want to move from dateable to mateable, it won't happen unless they value being mateable. Recognizing the very notion of being mateable is the first step in moving toward that goal. Other actions that can be taken to facilitate this movement include:

◇ Acknowledging where you're currently located on the continuum
◇ Living some of the Spiritual Wisdoms
◇ Seeing the movement you wish to make as a serious shift or life transition
◇ Asking yourself what you're giving up by becoming mateable

MATEABLE

The following are the basic qualities of mateable people:

◇ Consider romantic friendship to be the foundation of a relationship
◇ Want but don't need to be in a relationship
◇ Have realistic work commitments
◇ Keep their life in balance
◇ Have a good network of friends
◇ See romance and sex as a part of a relationship, not the whole relationship
◇ Are there in good and bad times

⋄ Move consciously, slowly, and consistently to develop a mateable relationship
⋄ Are realistic about the type of relationship they want
⋄ Want for you what you want for yourself
⋄ Give time to the relationship
⋄ Act responsibly for themselves and their partner
⋄ Are monogamous
⋄ Make the other person an important part of their life
⋄ Take life seriously
⋄ Share the same values

As you're moving toward this mateable state, remember that you need to factor another person's dateable or mateable status into the equation of your relationship. A mateable individual combined with a dateable person doesn't add up to a mateable couple. Both of you need to be mateable, and it's important to evaluate where a prospective partner is on the continuum and his or her willingness to move toward the mateable end of the line. Once you're both there, you are able to form one of the three types of mateable relationships—companion, soul mate, or spiritual partnership. (As discussed in chapter 15.)

SOUL DATEWORK

In thinking about these questions, remember that you can't make a person change to mateable. No matter how much you like or even love someone, you can't convince him or her to become mateable. The process has to come from within that person and reflect his or her values.

1. At this moment, are you dateable or mateable? Make a list of what makes you dateable. Make a list of what makes you mateable.

2. Do you want to be mateable? What are you doing to move from dateable to mateable?

3. Think about someone you've dated in the past or are currently dating, and determine whether he or she is dateable or mateable. What makes this

person dateable? Where is he or she on the continuum? What makes this person mateable?

4. Identify a couple you know who has a mateable relationship. Ask them to describe it. What qualities does each person have that make them mateable?

MEDITATIONS

Dateable: *I acknowledge that I am dateable and embrace it without criticism or judgment. I know that when I'm ready I will move from dateable to mateable.*

Mateable: *I take great pleasure in being mateable and continue to prepare to meet my companion, soul mate, or spiritual partner, who is preparing to meet me.*

Soul Dating Step 8: Nonnegotiables

Nonnegotiables are the qualities that reflect your core values and are essential if you hope to find a companion, soul mate, or spiritual partner. They reflect both personality and soul qualities. They can be as pragmatic as refusing to date someone who is a nonsmoker, and as spiritual as desiring a partner who encourages you to reveal vulnerable parts of yourself.

23

Nonnegotiables are derived from what you value and what pushes your buttons. They are requirements that your head can spell out with certainty ("I will not go out with anyone who doesn't love the outdoors"). They are requirements that you feel in your heart and soul ("I want someone who, from the first moment, I feel like I've known forever").

In this section, we will help you not only define your nonnegotiables, but define them clearly. When you're vague about what your nonnegotiables are, you won't find what you want. To deny one nonnegotiable is to deny a major part of who you are. To ignore one quality means that you're willing to settle for someone who will fall short in some way. Without clarity, it's easy for romantic illusion to take hold. If you're not exactly sure what you need in a partner, you're dateable not mateable.

Soul dating is a step-by-step process, and never more so than in the area of nonnegotiables. The steps in the following pages are designed to help you define your personality and soul nonnegotiables and reflect with absolute clarity on the qualities that you will need in a partner to support your relationship choice—whether companion, soul mate, or spiritual partner. Follow these nonnegotiable soul dating steps slowly and consciously.

RECOGNIZE PARENTAL INFLUENCE

What do you really want and need from a partner?

The first thing that comes to mind may not be what's in your heart and soul. On the surface, creating a list of nonnegotiables may seem easy. But anyone who isn't conscious and doesn't follow the soul dating steps is likely to produce an incomplete or even inaccurate list.

Consider this scenario: You meet someone who sweeps you off your feet. The attraction is immediate and intense. Sooner or later, however, you realize you couldn't have made a worse choice. In fact, you may have made this same type of bad choice in other failed relationships.

Your inclination may be to beat yourself up over what you seem to want in a partner. Don't. Most of us make mistakes like this. It's not uncommon to create a false mental picture of an "ideal" partner. Our family histories and other factors make it likely that we'll do so. Nonnegotiables help us create a true picture. When we identify the external and internal qualities to which we resonate, that picture starts to come into focus.

We can't define our nonnegotiables without considering the impact our parents have on this definition. Some of us find it difficult to define what we want in a partner because we were taught as children that our needs weren't important. Some of us specify nonnegotiables that would please our parents; others list traits that would outrage them. All of our nonnegotiables, to a lesser or greater extent, have been shaped by early family relationships.

We need to become aware of our parents' beliefs versus our own. It may be that they're one and the same: they want you to marry a Catholic and you want to marry a Catholic. It could be that your personality nonnegotiables are similar to what your parents would have wanted, while your soul nonnegotiables are quite different.

We can't know what we really want in a partner until we identify what our parents wanted (or might have wanted, given their beliefs) for us. To give you a sense of how this is so, let us share Adrienne's experience with you.

Adrienne, a thirty-nine-year-old litigator and partner with a top law firm who had been divorced a few years earlier, described what she wanted in a partner in vague terms: "*good-looking, nice, common interests.*" *She had great difficulty being specific about the traits she desired. This uncertainty had resulted in a five-year "nonmarriage" to a sweet but dull man who drank too much. Since the divorce, Adrienne's inability to define what she wanted produced a series of charming but emotionally abusive men.*

When Adrienne was in junior high school, go-go boots were the rage. When she told her mother she wanted these boots, her mother replied, "Oh, you don't need them." Time after time, overtly and subtly, her mother and her father denied the importance of Adrienne's feelings. As an adult, Adrienne didn't trust her feelings, apologizing whenever she related a highly emotional experience.

The man Adrienne married conformed to her parents' specifications, not her own. Her parents feared assertive, sexual men and favored passive, asexual ones. After the divorce, her relationship choices were still influenced by her parents. She chose men who were the direct opposite of what her parents wanted for her, ending up with equally inappropriate partners.

Until Adrienne does her inner work—until she discovers the personality and soul traits that really matter to her—her choices in men will continue to reflect her parents' nonnegotiables rather than her own.

SOUL DATEWORK

Picture the kind of person your parents would have chosen for you. What emotional/spiritual/physical/financial and other characteristics would your partner have? Write a paragraph or list ten to fifteen of these qualities. Consider both the spoken and unspoken messages that were relayed to you.

MEDITATION

I acknowledge my parents' vision of my life partner and believe that their intent was loving and meant to support me. I need to discover, however, my own vision of my life and partner.

UNDERSTAND SOCIETAL INFLUENCE

What we may think we want and need in a partner is also influenced by societal messages regarding gender. Social norms may cause us to search for men who are "the strong, silent type" or women who are sweet and compliant. We believe we want these "ideals" because society tells us we should want them. Depending on your age and sex, you may be under the sway of other socially desirable gender types: the sensitive, caring male or the superwoman.

Complicating matters is the struggle between the sexes. Many of us have been brought up to believe that the differences between men and women are irreconcilable. We've been bombarded with messages suggesting that the differences are so great that it's difficult to find common ground. Instead of learning to understand and appreciate the differences between men and women, we let the differences cloud our perceptions. When we try and create our list of nonnegotiables, we are hampered by these erroneous beliefs and generalities.

SOUL DATEWORK

We can work on separating societal messages from our own true needs and desires by completing the following exercise. Read the list below of some common societal messages about gender. Which ones are familiar? Which ones influence you? What other societal messages affect how you view yourself and the opposite sex?

Men are smarter than women.
Women are overly emotional.
Men shouldn't cry.
Women nag.
Men know how to handle finances.
Women are naturally nurturing.
Men are more ambitious and serious about their careers.
Women care more about relationships than men do.
Men should be the ultimate breadwinners.
Women should never call a man.
Men should always pay for women on dates.
Women all want to be married.
Men do not want to commit.
Women want to have sex less often than men.
All men want is sex.
Men and women are in competition.

MEDITATION

I respect the differences between men and women. I continue to expand my admiration and appreciation of the opposite sex.

DETERMINE YOUR NEEDS AND VALUES

Once you understand the impact of parents and society on the people you're drawn to, you're ready to confront your own needs and values. Think about what your life would look like without a partner. That may seem strange—after all, most of us have been raised to consider our happiness as inextricably linked to a boyfriend or girlfriend, husband or wife. But seeing yourself only in relation to another person transfers much of the power for your happiness to someone else.

You need to be certain of your identity and life plan before adding a partner to your life. Unless you're clear about who you are from both soul and personality perspectives, you're unlikely to find a partner that supports you. Some people have difficulty conducting this self-exploration when they're single; they put their lives on hold, waiting to find someone to love. Not only do they refuse to take vacations, buy nice furniture, or take part in service activities, but they avoid contemplating what's meaningful to them, who they really are, and what motivates them. All this represents needy behavior.

Being single becomes an excuse for not taking control of their inner and outer lives. They turn into observers rather than fully engaged participants. When they identify their real interests, goals, and needs, however, they can enjoy rich and satisfying lives. The fact that this self-awareness leads them to their partner is simply a wonderful bonus.

Let's return to Adrienne and see how she approached these issues. We asked Adrienne to describe the life she really wanted; to give us a sense of her hopes and dreams, not her hopes and dreams related to a partner. We asked her to incorporate all aspects of her life into this description—both doing and being activities—and this is what she came up with:

I'd live in a warm, sunny climate—I get very depressed in the winter. And in a serene house with land and trees around it. I'd have two children and a nanny to help me take care of them. I don't feel I could handle kids alone. I'm afraid of being like my mother was—and overreact in love and anger. I know that's why I don't have children . . . but if I had someone there to help me balance things. . . . I'd still be an attorney, but my career would be more involved in promoting and supporting women. Financially, I would be where I am now: comfortable enough to travel three times a year and save some money for the future. . . . I'd like to be involved in some kind of cause or charity and do community theater—something I haven't done since high school. I guess I'd have more free time to develop my spiritual side. . . .

Though Adrienne enjoyed being an attorney, many of her needs were going unfulfilled. She was living in a city (Chicago) with a climate that was anything but warm and sunny, she lacked the time to do everything she wanted (including spending more time alone), and she was not involved with any charity or women's issues. She was living an unbalanced life that didn't represent what she really wanted.

We suggested to Adrienne that she consider practical ways to fulfill her goals. We came up with a number of ideas that would bring Adrienne closer to the reality she desired:

⋄ Transfer to her firm's Los Angeles or Miami office
⋄ Investigate ways she could take on cases that supported women's issues
⋄ Do *pro bono* work for women's groups
⋄ Learn how to delegate more of her work to associates so that she would have more free time to do what she wanted

SOUL DATEWORK

1. As Adrienne did, write a paragraph describing the life that supports who and what you are.

2. Are your dreams and desires being fulfilled? If not, what practical things could you do to fulfill your desires?

MEDITATION

I will consider all possible options open to me that will enrich my life, increase my possibilities, and create new opportunities. I will turn my realistic wants and needs into reality.

PARTNER REQUIREMENTS: FIRST LOOK

Translating what you desire in your life to what you require in a partner demands some inner work. You need to make the connection between how your life aspirations affect what you require in a partner. At first, you may find that you can only create a hazy picture. That's fine. Getting to know yourself is a gradual process. Give yourself the time and patience that this process deserves. Later you'll have the opportunity to create a more detailed "portrait" of your partner.

Adrienne struggled a bit with her first list of partner essentials. We asked her to think about the emotional, practical, and spiritual qualities that would help support the life she desired. She created the following list:

Willing to move to the South or West
Healthy lifestyle
Well-dressed
Professional
Educated
Wants to have children
Good sense of humor
Emotionally warm
Takes responsibility for his own actions and emotional health and well-being
Can talk about feelings
Has a sense of social contribution
Participates in activities that are meaningful to him
Values a life that embraces healthy living
Views women in a positive light
Supportive of me and my career

SOUL DATEWORK

Go back to the previous soul datework exercise and revisit the things in life that you deemed important to you. Ask yourself, "What kind of partner would I need to support this lifestyle?" Think about both personality and soul traits you desire in a partner and create a list.

MEDITATION

I am beginning to visualize the qualities that I must seek in a partner.

PARTNER REQUIEMENTS: A MORE SERIOUS LOOK

Now you're ready to take your first crack at a nonnegotiable list. Non-negotiables are your soul and personality requirements for a partner and evolve from what you value.

This isn't an easy step. We are often vague about what we really want in a partner. When we create a nonnegotiable list of generalized traits—"a nice person," "successful," and "friendly"—we won't attract or recognize the specific partner we need.

Clarity is critical. When we clearly define the type of person we want, we're much more likely to recognize that person when we meet him or her. Similarly, clear nonnegotiables help eliminate people who don't meet our specific requirements. From a spiritual standpoint, clear intention becomes energy and attracts like energy. Once we define and refine our nonnegotiable list, the right people start showing up in our lives.

In contrast, vague nonnegotiables give romantic illusion a foothold. Because we haven't clearly defined what we want and need, we're susceptible to the myths. When we're not specific about nonnegotiables, we substitute Hollywood and romance novel images. Because we're not sure who it is we want in a partner, we borrow the "tall, dark, and handsome" image or convince ourselves that it's love at first sight.

Nonnegotiables are serious stuff. They are not about creating a wish list of trivial traits and seeing if someone measures up. They identify the soul and personality characteristics you can't do without in a partner. There are no right or wrong characteristics. Your list will necessarily be idiosyncratic—your uniqueness demands that it be. You may also include qualities that strike others as silly or unimportant. "He must love my two cats and my dog" might seem ridiculous to someone who doesn't give a hoot about animals. To another, however, it represents a core value. Don't be swayed by what others consider important. Understand what your particular nonnegotiables are and don't settle for less. If you give up a nonnegotiable, you're giving up a vital part of who you are.

It's also important to consider both personality and soul traits. Most people begin their lists focusing on personality—on external qualities such as appearance, career, and hobbies of a partner. Society pushes us in this direction, and it's also easier to compile a list of external traits than internal ones. But don't neglect your emotional and spiritual sides! More so than personality qualities, these are the ones that will lead you to your soul mate or spiritual partner. In fact, they can sometimes redirect the requirements dictated by the personality. For instance, at the time Basha met Jeff, he had determined that he wanted a younger woman. When he listened to his higher self, he discovered what he really wanted was someone who was younger in spirit. Because Jeff listened to his soul rather than his personality, he started to date Basha who was close to his age.

If you're uncertain whether a nonnegotiable is a personality or a soul trait, put it to the "why test." In other words, ask why it's important to you. If the answer is an external ("I want someone who loves going to plays, gallery openings, and the opera because I enjoy being part of the social scene"), then it's grounded in personality. If the answer is an internal ("I want someone who loves going to plays, gallery openings, and the opera because my love of art defines who I am"), then it's related to the soul.

We have found that the characteristics most people tend to value fall into certain general categories. This is not the only way to organize the traits you feel are essential—nor is it exhaustive—but it is a helpful way to get started. Feel free to add more nonnegotiable categories or to eliminate them as you see fit. Most people will have at least one or more nonnegotiables under each general heading. Consider what you feel you need in a partner that supports who and what you are, as well as things you don't want. Following is a list of many common nonnegotiable categories.

NONNEGOTIABLE CATEGORIES

CAREER
  Educational background
  Income range
  Involvement—time, goals, contribution, satisfaction
  Professional/White collar/Blue collar
  Travel—how much

COMMUNICATION STYLE
  Accepting/Judgmental
  Direct/Indirect
  Intellectual/Emotional
  Verbal/Nonverbal

EMOTIONAL STYLE
  Conscious/Unconscious
  Deals with conflict
  Done emotional, psychological, and healing work
  Excitable/Reserved
  Inner- vs. other-directed
  Intimate
  Knows competencies and incompetencies
  Loud or quiet
  Moody
  Need for personal space
  Optimistic or pessimistic
  Planner/Spontaneous
  Self-confidence
  Sense of humor

FAMILY, FRIENDS, PETS
  Children (how many, natural, adopted, custody issues, etc.)
  Extended family
  Friends/Social Groups
  Pets—type, ownership, boarding, traveling

FINANCIAL STYLE
  Bank accounts, investments
  Bill paying
  Debts (credit cards, loans, mortgages)
  Spending (conservative/liberal)

HEALTH
  Addictions (drinking, drugs, food, gambling, work)

Diet
Drinking
Drugs (illegal, prescription)
Energy level
Exercise (type, time commitment)
HIV status (AIDS)
Medical care (type/frequency/checkups)
Medical history (cancer, STDs, etc.)
Mental health
Physical disabilities
Sleep habits (hours, early/late riser)
Smoking

INTERESTS, LEISURE, AND HOBBIES
Arts—fine art, music, theater, movies, TV
Community service
Dancing
Dining/Cooking
Environment/Nature
Hobbies—photography, games, collecting, etc.
Reading
Sports—participatory or spectator
Travel—vacation (types, frequency)
Workshops and seminars

PHYSICAL
Age range
Appearance
Height/Weight
Personal beauty or handsomeness
Personal hygiene

RELATIONSHIP STYLE
Gender roles
Personal/spiritual growth—theirs/yours
Satisfies others' needs—emotional, physical, psychological, spiritual
Time together vs. alone

SEXUAL STYLE
    Birth control (attitudes, preferred methods/safe sex)
    Heterosexual/Bisexual/Homosexual
    Monogamous/"Open relationships"
    Physically affectionate
    Playful
    Romantic
    Sensual
    Sexual intercourse (frequency)
    Traditional or experimental

SOCIAL AND CULTURAL
    Community involvement
    Politics (conservative/liberal)
    Race/Ethnicity

SPIRITUAL
    Connection to universe and a higher consciousness
    Five senses vs. multisensory
    Practices a spiritual lifestyle
    Sense of meaningfulness and purpose—here to learn lessons
    Trusts heart and intuition more than mind and intellect
    Values contribution

Adrienne worked hard on defining her nonnegotiables. Using the categories we've suggested, she came up with the following list:

ADRIENNE'S FIRST LIST OF NONNEGOTIABLES

CAREER
    professional/semiprofessional job
    college degree
    holds a steady job
    a go-getter

COMMUNICATION STYLE
  can discuss hard issues without judgment

EMOTIONAL STYLE
  not "needy"
  can identify and express his emotions
  doesn't "crazy-make"
  introspective
  encourages me in my career
  has a good sense of humor
  open attitude: not prejudiced because of race, ethnicity, gender, sexual
    preference
  planner, well organized

FAMILY, FRIENDS, PETS
  good relationship with his family
  wants to have one/two children
  open to hiring a full-time nanny
  has no young children or custody of older children
  enjoys cats

FINANCIAL STYLE
  lives within his means
  balances spending with saving

HEALTH
  nonsmoker
  nondrinker
  works out regularly
  moderate to high energy level
  willing to live in South/West; a suburb of a major city

INTERESTS AND LEISURE TIME
  likes sports and participates in them
  enjoys theater and movies
  enthusiastic about traveling

PHYSICAL

   demonstrates a concern for self-image

   clean, neat clothing

   youthfulness

RELATIONSHIP STYLE

   committed to working on the relationship

   views women in a positive light

   goes on inward retreats

   interested in being my friend as well as my lover

SEXUAL STYLE

   sensitive and affectionate

   romantic, gives gifts

   monogamous

   moderate frequency of sexual activity

SOCIAL AND CULTURAL

   knowledge about politics and current events

   politically liberal, open to social activism

SPIRITUAL

   works (hands-on) with a charity

SOUL DATEWORK

   *Your nonnegotiables may need to be refined several times as you en-
   counter new people and evolve in your spiritual growth.*

1. Review the nonnegotiable categories as well as Adrienne's list. Think about which traits under each subhead you would need to find in a life partner. Use your first list of partner essentials to get yourself started. Are all the things you mentioned in your first list really nonnegotiables? Have you struck a balance between soul and personality nonnegotiables? Do they reflect your relationship choice—companion, soul mate, or spiritual partner?

Using the nonnegotiable subheads as a guide, delete traits that are not true necessities and add qualities you may not have previously considered.

Most people have at least one nonnegotiable under each heading. If you have fewer than twenty or twenty-five nonnegotiables, it means you aren't clear about who you are and what's important to you. If you have more than seventy-five, you're being unrealistic and have probably eliminated some suitable partners from consideration. Don't get hung up on where you put a particular nonnegotiable. Just get it into one of the categories.

2. Another way of determining your nonnegotiables is to create two parallel lists: the first "nonnegotiables" and the second "preferences." For each nonnegotiable, ask yourself, "Is this something I *must* have to be true to myself? Or is it something I would like but is not essential?" Those that are not essential belong on your list of preferences.

MEDITATION

I take responsibility for my nonnegotiable list. I deserve all the qualities I'm asking for.

PARTNER REQUIREMENTS: EXPANDING YOUR LIST

When you create your list of nonnegotiables, be specific and descriptive. Many of our clients say they want someone "successful." We ask them: "What does that look like to you in the real world?" In other words, what would someone need to have achieved in order for you to identify her or him as successful? What kind of lifestyle would he or she have? How much money? What kind of behaviors?

We need to challenge our assumptions and pin ourselves down when we say we want someone who is "attractive" or "thoughtful." Only when we strip away the generalities and ask ourselves some probing questions can we determine what we feel is really important so we can recognize those qualities in another.

Adrienne needed to clarify a number of traits on her list. One of the traits—under the "Emotional Style" heading—was "introspective." The following dialogue is a condensed version of the questioning process that helped Adrienne better define the word and her specific needs.

Us: When you say "introspective," do you mean someone who spends a lot of time thinking about himself?

ADRIENNE: No, not exactly. I suppose I want someone who really thinks deeply about the issues in his life.

Us: Are you saying that you don't want someone who is superficial?

ADRIENNE: Yes, but that's not exactly it either. I've been with a number of guys who just barreled through life blissfully unaware of who they were and how they were affecting others. At the same time, I don't want some brooding, self-absorbed guy either.

Us: Try to describe what the person would be like in the real world. Would he be the sort of person who meditates and is into yoga? Would you prefer someone who has been through therapy?

ADRIENNE: What I think I'm really saying is I want someone who is in touch with his feelings, and I don't care if he's done that through therapy, meditation, or some other technique.

Adrienne crossed off "introspective" from her list and replaced it with "in touch with feelings."

SOUL DATEWORK

Revise your nonnegotiable list. You will probably want to add new traits. Think carefully about what soul qualities as well as personality traits you require. What does each nonnegotiable look like to you in the real world? Be specific and descriptive. If you had to explain what you meant to another person, how would you do it? These exercises may help:

1. Make a list of old relationships. Which parts worked? Which parts didn't?

2. Ask one or two couples whose relationships (companion, soul mate, or spiritual partner) you aspire to, what qualities they sought in their mate that enabled them to have the relationship they now have.

3. Consider your relationships with same- or opposite-sex friends. Are there similarities in traits that seem consistent in people you admire and with whom you relate? Which qualities do you enjoy in different people? What feels good? What doesn't?

4. Pay attention to your lifestyle. What time do you normally eat, sleep, work? Are you a day person or a night owl? Neat or messy? About which areas of your schedule are you flexible? Which aspects are carved in stone? Do you lead a balanced life with both being and doing activities?

MEDITATION

The clearer I am about my nonnegotiables, the closer I come to finding my companion, soul mate, or spiritual partner.

PARTNER REQUIREMENTS: FINE-TUNING

You deserve to find a person who meets your nonnegotiables. You can choose not to date or enter a relationship until you have found someone who reflects your value system. Sooner or later, you'll find your companion, soul mate, or spiritual partner if your nonnegotiables are detailed, descriptive, and complete.

The last step in this section is designed to help you expand and explain the traits on your list. Use the description of past relationships from the previous soul datework exercise to refine your list. The problems and possibilities raised by past relationships are good guides for fine-tuning your nonnegotiables. You can take cues from people in your past and let what you learn shape the traits you place on your list.

Keep in mind that this list isn't final. As you date, you will be given opportunities to "test" your nonnegotiables against real-world experiences. Being "in the field" (dating) is where you have a hands-on opportunity to get clarity about them.

Adrienne put her list under close scrutiny, adding more detail about the qualities she desired as well as coming up with a number of new ones. Focusing on past relationships greatly assisted her in this process. Because Adrienne was passionate about women's issues and had been involved with men who put her down, she knew that a top priority was a partner who viewed women positively. When we pushed her to tell us how she could identify such a person, she talked about how a man's relationship with his mother would be a good indicator. "It seems like a lot of the men I've gone out with hated their mothers," she explained. "I think it makes sense to insist on someone who has a positive relationship with his mother."

After a good deal of introspection and dating, Adrienne realized she was looking for a companion on the continuum to a soul mate relationship and came up with the following "new and improved" list:

ADRIENNE'S REVISED NONNEGOTIABLE LIST

CAREER
holds at least a bachelor's degree
professional/semiprofessional job
holds a steady job and has a regular income
understands that success means more than making money
can make less money than I do, but is self-sufficient financially and not
   intimidated by my salary
has a job that he finds meaningful and loves

COMMUNICATION STYLE
can discuss hard issues without judgment
vulnerable issues don't come back to be used against me
will keep an open mind on all issues

EMOTIONAL STYLE
encourages me in my career
  - accepts that my career is valuable and time-consuming

- does not expect me to be home every night for dinner, or to cook more than twice a week
- willing to go to law firm functions when appropriate
- no snide remarks, cuts, subtle jabs that devalue what I do

not "needy"
- doesn't reveal at the beginning of dating every insecurity known to man
- doesn't blame everyone else for his problems
- doesn't instantly assume a relationship has begun just because we have dated a few times

can identify and express his emotions
- can express in words his happiness, sadness, etc.
- is willing to talk about what is bothering him
- is willing to discuss his emotions and feelings
- doesn't show physical discomfort when emotions rise (pacing, fidgeting, etc.)

doesn't "crazy-make"
- doesn't use passive-aggressive behavior to control a situation or the relationship
- does not play "uproar"
- accepts responsibility and doesn't blame me when things go wrong

is introspective
- seeks answers to questions about his emotional makeup
- has a sense of how his family influenced his life both positively and negatively
- can express his emotions so that I can understand him—not just the "buzz words"

open attitude—doesn't make derogatory remarks about people's race, ethnicity, gender, or sexual preference; no ethnic "jokes"

planner, well organized

FAMILY, FRIENDS, PETS
mother (has a good relationship with her)
- can spend time with her and enjoy it
- cares deeply for her, but is not controlled by her (whether she is alive or deceased)

- uses positive and compassionate adjectives when describing her
- knows when her birthday is and buys her gifts

other family members (has a good relationship with them)

- same indicators as above

open to hiring a full-time nanny

enjoys cats

children

- does not have primary custody of children; has no children under the age of 12
- has a close relationship with his children (not to serve his needs)
- no children who are unusual financial/emotional burdens (practicing addicts, severely physically or mentally ill)
- willing to have at least one child with me

FINANCIAL STYLE

lives within his means

saves part of his salary every month, but is willing to treat himself and me

conservative about investments

pays off his charge cards monthly and does not have debts that can't reasonably be paid off without stress to our lifestyle (car, mortgage, etc.)

HEALTH

nonsmoker

moderate drinker—some social drinking acceptable (0–2 drinks in a social setting, an occasional drink with dinner)

does some form of exercise on a regular basis (brisk walks, jogs, Stairmaster 2–3 times per week, within reason)

watches diet (limits red meat, fried food, fat, salt, and sugar intake), not a compulsive eater

acknowledges mental health by setting aside time for relaxation

gets regular physical exams

moderate to high energy level

willing to live in South/West; a suburb of a major city

INTERESTS AND LEISURE TIME

likes sports and participates in them

enjoys theater and movies

values "being" activities, such as meditation and yoga

reads books and goes to personal growth seminars

chooses to travel on a regular basis

PHYSICAL

clean, neat, stylish clothing

no really out-of-date or tacky fashions

will dress appropriately for my client/firm functions (i.e., in a suit)

5 years younger to 10 years older (some flexibility, depending on health, maturity)

no more than 25–30 pounds overweight

RELATIONSHIP STYLE

views women in a positive light

- speaks about women as capable human beings
- doesn't use subtleties to "put a woman in her place"
- can describe the personalities of women, not just physical attributes
- has a track record of being respectful to women and liking them
- does not "bash" former girlfriends/wife
- has a track record of not cheating on women, is monogamous
- not a "womanizer" (i.e., taking great pride in "scoring big" in bed)

is committed to our relationship

- is willing to talk about the good and the bad
- doesn't retreat from the relationship on a frequent basis
- provides strategies for solving problems in the relationship
- is willing to invest time to enhance the relationship; doesn't just leave the relationship to "chance"

interested in being my romantic friend as well as lover

- knows the important elements that create friendship (time, understanding, support, listening)
- has solid and long-standing friendships with two or more people
- realizes that closeness to a person goes beyond a sexual relationship

SEXUAL STYLE

    has a balanced desire to be with me

    is sensitive and affectionate as well as sexual

    tells me he cares about me with both words and actions (does small
        favors for me, treats me sometimes just because . . .)

    remembers my birthday and gives me gifts that reflect an understanding
        of me

    can hug and kiss and does so often

    believes in foreplay and isn't inhibited about oral sex

    cares about my sexual needs and can express his

    is willing to try new things

    does not "withhold" sex when angry

    accepts my body as it is

SOCIAL AND CULTURAL

    politically moderate to liberal, open to social activism

    can converse about well-known books, plays, and literary, historical, or
        political figures

    keeps abreast of current political and cultural affairs

SPIRITUAL

    works (hands-on) with a charity

    has his personality and soul aligned

    values the spiritual and not just the material

Marv's list is another example of a well-thought-out set of nonnego-tiables. This list is different from Adrienne's because it reflects someone who has done a good deal of inner work, lives the Spiritual Wisdoms, and is working toward a spiritual partnership.

MARV'S NONNEGOTIABLES AND PREFERENCES

CORE PERSONALITY, SPIRITUAL ESSENCE

This woman is passionate about life and it shows! She exudes a joie de vivre (joy of living) that is reflected in many ways. You can see it in her positive and optimistic outlook. She views herself as the master of her own fate and accepts responsibility for herself. She has an adventurous spirit and enjoys trying and doing new things. She's fun-loving, playful, and loves to laugh. She is also affectionate—to her, touching, hugging, cuddling, and kissing are natural and fundamental forms of sharing warmth in a relationship.

PHYSICAL

Nonnegotiables

Attractive to me

Warm smile and a happy laugh

Weight reasonable for height (neither very overweight nor emaciated)

Bonus points:

Petite (shorter than 5'5")

Long, straight black hair

Oval face, high cheekbones

Olive to dark complexion

32–40 years old

Sleeps an average of 6 hours/night (or less)

Doesn't use a lot of makeup

HEALTH AND FITNESS

Nonnegotiables:

Physically fit

Nonsmoker

Moderate drinking (e.g., wine with dinner out; 2–3 drinks at party)

Not food-obsessive (e.g., constant dieting)

Not a junk food junkie (e.g., seldom eats McDonald's, Burger King)

Bonus points:
  Exercises regularly (3 to 6 times/week)
  Runner
  Step aerobics
  Rock climbing
  Weight training
  Early-morning workouts

EMOTIONAL

Nonnegotiables:
  Positive and optimistic outlook
  Accepts responsibility for herself
  Comfortable with and emotionally secure in her identity
  Likes herself (high self-esteem)
  Affectionate, not uptight about public affection
  Open and able to share feelings, emotions, and vulnerabilities
  Flexible and spontaneous (can cope with last-minute changes)
  Not super-moody, generally even-keeled
  Easygoing, calm, usually happy
  Not often angry, frustrated, depressed (and down moods pass quickly)
  Neither selfish nor selfless
  Able to give and receive love
  Considerate and sensitive to others' feelings and needs
  Compassionate, kind, and giving of herself
  Not manipulative or controlling
  Not a victim
  Able to be alone without being lonely

Bonus points:
  Sentimental (e.g., teary-eyed at end of emotional film)

RELATIONSHIP

Nonnegotiables:
  Ready for a healthy, committed relationship
  Best friends
  Equal partners (neither subservient/superior)
  Spends time working on the relationship
  Supportive, share vulnerabilities and guard each other's secrets

Can tell each other everything
Major decisions are joint decisions (finances, vacations, etc.)
Split/share responsibilities such as cleaning, laundry, groceries
Balance between being together and being apart

Bonus points:
Prefers marriage (as opposed to living together)
She cooks (I'll clean up and wash the dishes)

FRIENDS, FAMILY, CHILDREN, PETS

Nonnegotiables:
Loves kids
Values home and family
Had a relatively happy childhood
Healthy relationship with her family
Wants good relations with my family and closest friends
Has at least 1 close friend and a social support group
Likes animals and must be willing to inherit my cat
Any current children are not teenagers (younger/older are O.K.)

Bonus points:
Wants to have 1 or 2 more children if she already has some

SOCIAL AND CULTURAL

Nonnegotiables:
Passionate about life and lives it fully
Honest, trustworthy, reliable, and dependable
Fun-loving and playful
Loves people and enjoys socializing
Down to earth (not a snob; doesn't put on false airs)
Good sense of humor and loves to laugh
Welcomes new experiences
Confident and comfortable in most situations
Not bigoted or racist, accepting of all cultures
Has good manners (e.g., uses please and thank you when appropriate)
Appreciates her cultural upbringing and heritage
Believes in giving to the community

Bonus points:

Prefers casual social situations (happier in jeans than dresses)

COMMUNICATION

Nonnegotiables:

Open, honest, and direct communicator (assertive)
Articulate (expresses thoughts so they're understood by others)
Good listener
Able to give and receive feedback
Committed to negotiate and resolve differences in a win-win fashion
Compatible fighting style—quick to boil but quickly dissipated
Speaks up when she has something to say (not afraid to be heard)
Can share and discuss feelings, wants, needs

Bonus points:

Skilled in techniques such as reflection and restatement
Enunciates clearly and not prone to dis, dat, dese, and dose
Writes well
Doesn't swear much and helps me to do the same

INTELLECTUAL

Nonnegotiables:

Intelligent and uses common sense
Fascinated by life and loves learning new things
Comfortable with the complexity of the Universe
Ongoing growth and self-improvement but not obsessed with it
Balance between goal orientation and living in the present
Realistic sense of self, including positive and negative attributes
Open-minded and respectful of others' points of view
Interesting to talk with
Not obsessed with politics or government

Bonus points:

Quick-witted
Comfortable with both deductive logic and intuitive thinking
Has a good memory

SEXUAL

Nonnegotiables:

Loves to hug, cuddle, and kiss (in and out of bedroom)
Sensual, luxuriates in touching and being touched
Romantic (cards, verbal affection, unexpected expressions of love)
Enjoys sex and is not inhibited or hung up about it
Open to some experimenting with ways to keep things exciting
Brings her sense of playfulness to the bedroom
Considerate lover, interested in mutual pleasing and satisfaction
Heterosexual
Monogamous and no history of promiscuity (cheating)

Bonus points:

Likes to give massages
Sometimes likes to be the initiator of sexual relations

PROFESSIONAL AND FINANCIAL

Nonnegotiables:

Maintains good balance between work, relationship, and play
Honest and ethical in business dealings
Money is not the goal but only a means to achieving other things
Balances earning, spending, saving, investing, sharing money
Thrifty (e.g., shops for best value on medium to expensive items)
Not a penny-pincher (e.g., buy paper only if can get it at discount)
Not secretive about finances
Home, office, and life are more organized than chaotic

Bonus points:

Happy and satisfied with the work she does
Financially secure
Can take the lead in retirement planning
Entrepreneurial spirit
Professional occupation

SPIRITUAL AND RELIGIOUS

Nonnegotiables:

Spiritual, believes in a universal force or power greater than us

Comes from a multisensory perspective
Is guided by soul not personality
Respects all life, the earth, and environment
Knows right from wrong and lives a moral, principled life
Compassionate for those who are less fortunate
Not very religious (not a weekly church/synagogue attender)
Not a member or participant in any cult
Willing to raise our children in the Jewish faith

Bonus points:
Is Jewish

INTERESTS AND HOBBIES

Nonnegotiables:
Share a good number of interests (likely 10 or more listed below)
Varied pursuits, including active, quiet, social, and solo activities
Adventurous and enjoys trying new things
Likes dining out 1–2 nights/week
Not a TV jock (not hooked on lots of TV sports)

Bonus points:
Running
Step aerobics
Rock climbing
Weight training
Science fiction
Stimulating conversations
Ethnic food (double bonus for spicy ethnic food)
Good wine with dinner out
Indian art
Travel (double bonus for weekend getaways)
Backpacking and hiking
Movies
Plays (theater)
Flea markets
Garage sales
Leisurely walks
Quiet reflective moments

Meditation
Yoga (current or desire to try)
Antique books and furniture
Bicycling
Scuba diving (current or desire to try)
White-water rafting/canoeing
Reading
Museums
Zoos
Computers
Bowling
Prefers warm-climate vacations

SOUL DATEWORK

The more specific or clear you are about your nonnegotiables, the easier it will be to find the appropriate partner. Remember, if you give up a nonnegotiable, you can never make your partner wrong for having this characteristic.

1. Revise your nonnegotiable list, using Adrienne's and Marv's lists as guidelines. See if there's anything that you've inadvertently forgotten to include or if you can be more specific and focused in describing certain traits.

2. Go out and date using the concepts of nonnegotiables, dateable vs. mateable and the type of relationship that you desire (companion, soul mate, spiritual partner) to guide you.

3. As you continue to date, you will be adding, omitting, and refining the traits on your list. This is a process you will revisit many times before finalizing your nonnegotiable list.

MEDITATION

I have the courage to date with my nonnegotiable list as my guiding force, knowing that consciousness and clarity will direct me to my companion, soul mate, or spiritual partner.

Soul Dating Step 9: Rejection

24

For most people, the fear of being rejected or rejecting someone else sets up barriers to dating. We've been taught that rejection is bad and that when we are rejected, it's because something's wrong with us.

This fear is powerful and paralyzing. It prevents us from asking people out, from saying what we truly believe, and from moving forward. We've also had many clients who were so afraid of rejection that they took themselves out of the dating scene before other people had a chance to meet them. Self-rejection translates into negative self-talk, such as "I'm not attractive enough" or "That person would never talk to me."

The irrational myth is that no one should get rejected. Therefore, most people do anything in their power to avoid rejection. By this traditional definition, rejection does hurt. It hurts when someone turns you down for a date, fails to ask you out, or breaks off a relationship. It's also painful to reject someone else; it's not easy to experience another person's disappointment when you say no.

We can't avoid rejection—it's part of the dating experience. If we become stuck in our fear of being hurt or hurting someone else, we will miss the dating opportunities that can lead to committed, meaningful relationships.

To avoid getting hurt, let's redefine rejection as reflecting the rejector's value system rather than indicating something is wrong with the rejectee. In fact, rejection has less to do with our perceived flaws and more to do with the other person's nonnegotiables. In other words, all of us reject people based on our nonnegotiables, our dateable/

mateable status, and the type of relationship (companion, soul mate, spiritual partner) we desire.

In the heat of the moment of rejection, however, it's tough to remember that rejection is not personal. This is what you need to say to yourself:

He's not rejecting me—he's honoring his nonnegotiables. I'm a worthwhile person and don't want to be with someone who doesn't value who I am.

Also, keep the following ideas in mind to help you through these difficult moments:

- ◊ Don't beat yourself up or take the rejection personally.
- ◊ Recognize that you can't be all things to all people.
- ◊ Acknowledge the loss; admit that you feel sad about the loss of the possibility.
- ◊ Realize that you'll meet other people, many of whom will be more appropriate for you than the one who rejected you.

Think of rejection as a gift, one that frees you to find someone who is better able to meet your needs. Unfortunately, we're often as afraid to give this gift as we are to receive it. If we embrace the idea that rejection is based on nonnegotiables, we'll feel less reticent to decline someone, and less reluctant of the awkwardness and embarrassment of breaking off a relationship. If we continue to go out with people whom we know we should reject, we're not doing them or ourselves any favors. We simply lock ourselves into dates that go nowhere and lock ourselves out of dating opportunities that would lead us to our partner.

To learn how to decline—to caringly say no to another person (which is a soulful approach)—you need to realize that most people would prefer a straight, truthful response rather than ambiguity or words that give them false hope. They may be disappointed if you tell them no, but they'll probably prefer the truth to the "I'll call you" lie. Rejecting others is a way of setting boundaries for yourself. It's an acknowledgment that some people are appropriate for you and others are not.

One of the reasons we don't reject others is that we don't know how to. How do you tell someone that you don't want to date him? There are compassionate ways of saying no. Here are some suggestions:

◇ *Make it clear you're talking about your value system.* It has nothing to do with them.

◇ *Don't try to make the other person understand.* Don't get caught up in helping someone you're rejecting understand the logic of the rejection. Don't try to convince them that this is the best thing for them. The more you try to explain and rationalize, the more difficult it is to carry it through (and the easier it is to be talked out of your rejection).

◇ *Say no in a clear, firm manner.* Avoid ambiguity, self-justification, and other approaches that muddy the waters. If there's no mistaking the no in your rejection, you won't give the other person false hope. Don't "soften" the blow by saying, "We can still be friends" and lead the other person to believe that there's still a chance.

◇ *Don't blame the other person or yourself.* Keep your words and your tone as kind, compassionate and warm as possible.

People sometimes have difficulty finding the right words to say no. Keep in mind that it's very important you give a reason to the rejectee so he or she understands that you're talking about *your* value system and it has nothing to do with him or her. The following are some examples of soulful, kind, straightforward, and compassionate ways to reject:

"Thanks for asking, but our goals aren't the same (or we don't have enough in common)."

"We're not a good match because I need someone who is athletic and enjoys the outdoors."

"No, thank you, I don't date _____(smokers, anyone who isn't Catholic, someone who wants children, etc.)."

"Thanks for asking, and I hope you meet someone who's right for you."

This one might be for someone you have dated several times:

"I've really enjoyed spending time with you but I realize that this isn't going to go beyond a platonic friendship, even though we've had some good communication. I don't feel a connection strong, and realize in many areas our values (nonnegotiables) are quite different."

Consider this example of a healthy rejection that Gail personally experienced many years ago:

Michael and Gail met at a party and felt an instant attraction. They made a coffee date for the next week. Michael, a fifty-two-year-old divorced doctor, shared that he regularly volunteered at a crisis hotline, had recently come back from a ski trip, and meditation was part of his daily routine. Gail revealed that she was an avid reader, loved to travel, taught fourth grade at a suburban school, and periodically took week-long retreats. The more they talked, the more they realized how much they had in common.

Michael went on to explain that he'd married late. After his divorce, he became the custodial parent of his four- and six-year-old sons. Gail's heart sank. She was at a stage in her life where she was very clear that she didn't want any strong ties to young children. She valued her carefree, unhampered lifestyle. When Michael asked her out again, regretfully she declined. She carefully explained that while she found him attractive and very interesting, she was clear that any man she started dating had to be unencumbered with children. Dating him would definitely mean compromising a very important nonnegotiable. Michael, while taken aback with Gail's candor, thanked her for her honesty. He told her he regretted not having the chance to get to know her better, but respected her for being clear and direct. He said it was the nicest rejection he'd ever received.

Whether you're doing the rejecting or being rejected, rejection can take place on the first date, after a few dates, or well into a relationship. Remember, some nonnegotiables take months to determine. Certainly the later it comes in the relationship, the more discussion needs to take place to work through the ending. But whenever it takes place, the reasons behind the rejection have to do with either the rejector's nonnegotiables, or her or his dateable/mateable status, or his or her choice of the type of relationship he or she values.

Keep in mind that rejection is a learning experience. If, for instance, you're being rejected frequently, what does it tell you? Don't answer that question judgmentally. Instead, consider if your behavior or style is turning people off. It may be that you're exhibiting needy behavior, picking inappropriate people, or under the spell of romantic illusion. If you're rejected often, look for the pattern in the rejection. If you're still unclear about why you are getting rejected, even though it might be painful, ask for direct feedback. Use what you learn to move inward, to reflect, to seek help, and to learn new ways to get the results you want.

SOUL DATEWORK

Rejection can actually be a healthy and learning aspect of the soul dating process.

1. Try to get rejected. Ask different people out. Encourage someone to ask you out. The only way to overcome your fear of being rejected (and the accompanying inertia) is to experience it. While you may have been rejected before, we're asking you to experience it with a new consciousness based on our definition. When you're rejecting or get rejected, say to yourself, "They're (I'm) honoring their (my) nonnegotiables and beliefs." Recognize that this rejection will move you closer to the dates you want to have or to your potential partner.

2. Memorize the kind ways of rejecting people found on pages 170–171. When an opportunity presents itself and a specific rejection is needed, try it out. Concentrate on being compassionate. Remember, you're giving the other person (as well as yourself) more opportunities to meet the right people.

MEDITATION

◇ *I love and respect myself and when I am rejected, I admire that person for being honest and honoring his or her values and nonnegotiables. It only means I have yet to find someone who appreciates my inner and outer beauty.*

◇ *I value each person's dignity and self-worth and when rejecting others, I will do so with kindness and compassion.*

Soul Dating Step 10: Interviewing

When evaluating the many issues that concern people about finding a mateable partner, a couple of essential questions need to be asked:

- How do I know if the person's right for me? I know I need to like the person, not just love them.

- Is each of my nonnegotiables truly essential for me to establish a mateable relationship?

- Are our nonnegotiables compatible? Do they support both our personality and our soul?

It's difficult to read some people. A few may deceive you, while others are out of touch with who they are. Sometimes we want so much for a person to meet all our requirements that we slip into romantic illusion and deceive ourselves. It's possible to assess some nonnegotiables with direct questions. Most require a series of questions, dialogues, and weeks or months of observing behaviors and responses to mutual sharing.

We've designed an interviewing process to help people deal with these issues. When we refer to interviewing, we're talking about something quite different from what goes on in a job interview. Instead of a two-way interrogation, it's an ongoing process that will help you evaluate:

- If you want to go out with someone for the first time
- If you want to continue to date this person
- If you want to enter into a committed relationship

◇ If this person has the capacity to be a companion, soul mate, or spiritual partner

This process starts with the first date and continues until you stop seeing the person or you decide he's your companion, soul mate, or spiritual partner. When you first start dating, it's important to date one date at a time. On each date, you're consciously assessing whether or not you want to go out on the next. It's important that you stay focused in the present and not jump into the future. During this time, be aware that it's easier to stop the relationship sooner rather than later; breaking up becomes more painful as time goes on.

Your style of interviewing is up to you and based on who you are. We've worked with people who are very playful and inventive in their interviewing, while others are more serious and direct. While the style may vary, the ingredients of the process remain constant:

◇ Asking questions to discover if a person meets your nonnegotiables
◇ Determining if someone is dateable or mateable
◇ Assessing whether the person lives the Spiritual Wisdoms and has done inner work
◇ Establishing if someone wants or is ready for the kind of relationship you want
◇ Observing nonverbal body language for responsiveness, attentiveness, and so on
◇ Paying attention to both what people reveal and what they conceal
◇ Picking up information from seeing where and how a person lives
◇ Engaging in dialogue and observing behavior that help you find out if the other person is emotionally safe
◇ Paying attention to what you hear rather than what you want
◇ Asking personal questions and sharing vulnerables
◇ Revealing intimate information about yourself to see how the other person responds

Can you do all this without the conscious process of interviewing? Absolutely not! Most people easily slip into romantic illusion, make false assumptions about the person they're dating, and make mistakes because they haven't taken time to assess their potential partner. Interviewing keeps us alert for signs of needy behavior. It also helps us determine how much inner work the person has done or is doing on himself and if he values and lives the Spiritual Wisdoms. It allows us to perceive who another person really is even if he doesn't consciously know himself. Interviewing also increases our awareness of ourselves.

We've found that some people resist interviewing, preferring to date in an "unconscious" manner. In one sense, this resistance is understandable. Interviewing doesn't always feel romantic, and romantic illusion provides a pulse-pounding (though temporary) rush of excitement that interviewing helps to prevent. Because having sex makes it difficult to interview objectively, we also ask people to refrain from it until at least three months into the interviewing process.

We find that this last request meets with a great deal of resistance. Though resistance to not having sex is understandable, it can be reduced if you start thinking about long-term relationships rather than short-term thrills. Interviewing is a necessary part of the path toward finding a relationship that supports you, and there aren't any shortcuts. Questioning, and revealing, help you discover important aspects of another person and yourself that you might otherwise miss.

Though asking the right questions certainly is important, just as important in interviewing is expressing your feelings and revealing your vulnerabilities. A vulnerability is a piece of information or a feeling that carries an emotional charge—it can range from a low emotional charge (low vulnerability) to a high one (high vulnerability). By revealing these vulnerabilities, we can learn a great deal about other people and allow them to learn about us. We can see if others value our emotional openness or are threatened by it. We can determine if they're emotionally safe. We can also gauge whether they're interested in hearing about more than just surface issues and accept our deeper emotional and soul concerns. Revealing our authentic self through these vulnerabilities, we give the people we date permission to do the same thing with us.

People respond to statements that reveal vulnerability (we call such statements vulnerables) in all sorts of ways, and it's important to pay attention to how they respond. At one end of the spectrum, they may try to talk you out of your vulnerables or even use them against you. At the other extreme, they may listen intently and encourage you to share these vulnerables, thus demonstrating their emotional safety.

Let's say you share a low vulnerable such as "I had a bad day today."

An emotionally safe response from your date would be "I'm really sorry. Do you want to tell me more about it? Believe me, I understand, since I've had days when I've just been incredibly overwhelmed too."

Unsafe responses include "Cheer up, tomorrow will be better," or "You think you had a bad day, just listen to mine," or "So what else is new?"

It's important that you escalate from low to medium to high vulnerables. It's possible that a person who is supportive with a low vulnerable may grow uneasy with a medium vulnerable like "I feel like a lot of people don't like me," or "I've been married twice." It may be that someone you're dating is fine with the medium vulnerables but freaks out when you reveal a high one such as "I have a history of depression," "I see auras," or "I'm a recovering drug abuser." Using the low, medium, and high levels as a barometer, you can learn what level of intimacy and emotional safety another person provides and whether that is good enough for you.

As you interview, it's also important to keep your nonnegotiables in mind. Let's take a simple example of how this evaluation works.

One of your nonnegotiables is being with a nonsmoker, someone who will honor your refusal to allow smoking in your presence and your intolerance of any environment where people smoke. During the interviewing process, you want to determine if someone will honor this nonnegotiable. If a date says, "It's not that important. You're making too big an issue out of it," or is perfectly content to stay at a smoke-filled party and ignore your request to leave, then you know he or she won't support your nonnegotiable.

Let's say you want to get a sense if someone you're dating is in tune with the following soul mate nonnegotiable: "I want to be with someone who will help me become a better, more evolved person." To interview for this nonnegotiable, you might share an issue you're struggling with and see if he is supportive and understands as you wrestle with the issue or if he can help you problem-solve. You should also observe whether he judges, criticizes, or acts as if his solution were the only right one. You would watch to see if his answers and behaviors indicate he can show you both sides of an issue; that he's interested in helping you learn and grow; that he's able to do so by allowing you to see yourself from a fresh perspective. Does he criticize you in order to get you to change or does he accept who you are and open you to ideas and feelings that allow you to change on your own?

Interviewing might take six months to a year from the first date until you know that someone is your life partner. It depends on how well each person knows him- or herself and how skilled both are at this process.

INTERVIEWING FOR A COMPANION

When interviewing for a companion, focus on personality rather than soul nonnegotiables—on externals such as attractiveness, money, career, family, children, similar goals, friendship, compatibility, and communication. As you interview, you should assess whether the person has a well-developed sense of her I.

It's important to recognize a potential companion's limits when interviewing. Keep in mind, a companion will not embrace all the Spiritual Wisdoms or value personal growth. She has not dealt with emotional wounds from her past and does not value communicating about emotional issues. All this is fine, but you need to look at companions realistically in order to avoid romantic illusion.

PERSONALITY QUESTIONS

⋄ What type of vacations do you like?
⋄ How do you spend your free time?
⋄ Are you looking for a long-term relationship? Marriage?
⋄ Do you enjoy your work?
⋄ Do you want children? How important is this to you?
⋄ Do you have a good relationship with your parents? With your siblings?
⋄ What are your interests?
⋄ Why did your most serious relationship end?
⋄ If you could have the perfect life, what would it look like?
⋄ What would you do with a three-million-dollar lottery jackpot?

INTERVIEWING FOR A SOUL MATE

While you would certainly interview for companion qualities if you're seeking a soul mate relationship, right from the start you would concentrate more on looking for soulful qualities such as an ability to share intimate concerns and low vulnerabilities. A soul mate interviewer needs to establish if the other person:

◇ Has done emotional and spiritual work and wants to continue this work as a couple
◇ Is committed to your and his or her own personal growth
◇ Values inventing the we and works on improving the relationship
◇ Wants to include you in what's meaningful in his or her life
◇ Values emotional intimacy
◇ Owns strengths and inadequacies and won't make you wrong for yours
◇ Lives the Spiritual Wisdoms individually and in the partnership
◇ Deals with issues—especially problems—directly and authentically
◇ Is conscious of his or her higher self and relationship to the universe

Remember, soul mates experience an intense sense of connectedness from the moment they meet; they feel extraordinarily comfortable together. This doesn't mean, however, that your soul mate wants or is ready for a committed relationship. Interviewing helps you assess whether you:

◇ Meet each other's nonnegotiables
◇ Have done and want to continue to do work at the I and we levels
◇ Desire to be in a committed relationship

SOUL QUESTIONS

◇ Do you value personal growth and learning?
◇ What is your purpose in life?
◇ What personal issues do you struggle with?
◇ How do you spend being time?
◇ What kind of service enriches you?
◇ What are your life lessons?
◇ What makes you an emotionally safe person?

⬧ What five things do you like and dislike about yourself?

⬧ What are some meaningful experiences you have had?

⬧ What have you learned about yourself from your past relationships?

INTERVIEWING FOR A SPIRITUAL PARTNER

Interviewing between spiritual partners occurs on a different plane. It is an intuitive connection where both partners *just know* about each other. It's that simple. Suffice it to say, spiritual partners have a natural flow together. They have no need to show up looking good. Their soul connection is so strong, their relationship so intense, their sex so transcendent, that the interview process is almost automatic and takes place over a short period of time. The relationship is instantaneous and they're together forever.

SOUL DATEWORK

Remember, interviewing is the way to find out if your date meets your nonnegotiables.

1. In your past dating experiences, what has kept you from consciously interviewing?

2. When you first meet someone (or talk to the person on the phone), ask, "What do you think is really important for me to know about you?" Even if the other person doesn't ask you this same question, answer it for him or her.

3. Go back to each of your personality and soul nonnegotiables and make sure you have a clear idea of what each one looks like. Keep asking yourself, "Why is this important to me and how am I going to interview for it?"

4. List some low vulnerables you'd share when you start dating someone. As you get to know this person better, what medium and high vulnerables would you reveal?

5. What vulnerables has the person you've been dating shared with you?

6. Are you being sent any warning signals contradicting your nonnegotiables from what you're hearing or observing? Are you taking them seriously?

7. Create a series of questions to help you determine if someone will meet your nonnegotiables. Make a list of behaviors and attitudes you'd observe that would demonstrate they could meet these nonnegotiables. As you are dating, what would you have to observe to confirm that a person met your requirements? With these questions, attitudes, and behaviors in mind, also determine if that person is capable of developing the type of mateable relationship (companion, soul mate, spiritual partner) that you want. Use the personality and soul questions on pages 177 and 178–179 to help you do this datework activity. Don't forget that just asking these questions is insufficient. Your observation of someone's actions, behaviors, and attitudes over a period of time is essential.

MEDITATION

Dateable: *I consciously interview to learn more about myself and others.*

Mateable: *My heart is open to interviewing and being interviewed carefully and without judgment. I know that interviewing is the way to my life partner.*

Soul Dating Step 11: Dating More Than One Person at a Time

The notion of dating a variety of people at once might initially strike you as being at odds with our approach. After all, is there anyone who takes dating less seriously than the person who flits from one date to the next, who plays the field in a series of superficial encounters? The difference is that we're not recommending you date other people without seriousness or purpose. This step is part of a learning process that is necessary for finding a partner.

Dating a number of people simultaneously gives you the time and perspective to continue to learn about yourself. This is an opportunity to refine your nonnegotiable list, distinguish between dateable and mateable people, see if someone is capable of being a companion or soul mate, and become a proficient interviewer. Making an immediate and total commitment to someone early on in the relationship is an open invitation to romantic illusion. You lose your objectivity, you lose the opportunity to interview for your nonnegotiables, and you lose the ability to learn if someone is dateable or mateable. These nonnegotiables are a work-in-progress, and as such they need to be shaped and changed over time. The experience of going out with different people will help you determine if a given nonnegotiable is really as important as you originally thought. On the other hand, when you immediately fall in lust with one person and dismiss others, your single-minded focus prevents you from determining if he or she has failed to support your nonnegotiables.

Recently, Glenn met Anne and was immediately taken with her. After going out on five dates he was beginning to dis-

26

cover that they had a lot in common and she appeared to meet many of his nonnegotiables.

But knowing that it all felt too good to be true and that he might slip into romantic illusion, he went—as he put it—"into high gear" and started putting out feelers to meet other women. He knew that if it was going to be the real thing it had to play out over a period of months.

"What I learned over this last year of dating is I feel less vulnerable in knowing that all my eggs aren't in one basket. Seeing other women helps me keep some distance and not make Anne bigger than life."

Dating a variety of individuals gives you options and slows down the dating process to a reasonable pace. When we date one person, we run the risk of losing ourselves in the relationship. Our life can become unbalanced and we may operate out of a need ("This is all I can get") rather than choice. Frequently, we try to make something out of an unexplored, underdeveloped, "nothing" relationship. By dating a diverse group of people, we have the time and space to assess whether someone is emotionally safe and trustworthy. We're not pressured into entering a relationship prematurely because we know we have other options.

Dating a few people gives the opportunity to learn and practice the soul-work steps and dating skills we've described. If done properly, you'll feel desirable and learn a great deal about yourself and others. "Done properly" means dating a number of people but not sleeping with them.

If you're like many of our clients, you may initially resist dating more than one person at a time. Some people resist it because it seems impractical: "I have enough trouble getting one date; how in the world am I going to find two or three people to go out with?" People are often surprised at how easy it is to find others to date when they enter the process with an optimistic attitude. If you happen to be going out with only one person and haven't found someone else to date, at least keep an open mind about meeting others. Typically, we allow romantic illusion to shut our minds to others after we think we've met that one special someone. It's very important to be open to meeting others until we decide to date one person exclusively.

The other reason for resistance is that many people have difficulty telling their dates from the start that they want to go out with other people. It's awkward and embarrassing, especially when they've gone out with someone four or five times. So, how do you tell someone after you've decided to see each other again, that you want to go out with other people? Here's one way:

"As we're getting to know each other, I'm going to be dating other people and I suggest you do the same. In the past, I've gotten caught up in lust and jumped into relationships too quickly, before I've really gotten to know the person. The relationships fizzled and I was hurt. Even though I find you attractive, interesting, and want to continue to get to know you, I know that dating more than one person will help me slowly develop a romantic friendship and not have unrealistic expectations. If we come to a point in our dating where we both want to take it to a more serious, committed level, we'll talk about it and decide together to stop dating other people."

As you start dating a number of people, the odds are that you'll run into dateable/mateable "conflicts." Ideally, if you're mateable and you meet a dateable individual, you'll stop dating that person when you determine his dateable status. Realistically, however, some of you who are mateable will continue to go out with dateable people because they help you lead a balanced life, keep romantic illusion at bay, and are just plain fun to be with. Though we don't recommend this mix, make sure you're clear and direct about your status. This will help you both make choices that don't surprise and hurt each other.

If the situation is reversed—you're dateable and the other person is mateable—it's also important to be honest and aboveboard about your status and that you're going to date others.

SOUL DATEWORK

Dating more than one person can require an attitude adjustment.

1. Whether you're dateable or mateable, how do you feel you would benefit from dating a number of people simultaneously? What nonnegotiables on your list are you learning more about? List them.

2. Answer this question: Why would I stop dating others before I've decided to become exclusive with one person?

3. As you date, do you explain your dateable or mateable status to your dates? If not, why not?

4. Are you resistant to dating more than one person at a time and having your dates do the same? Examine your reasons. Does it have to do with a lack of self-confidence and self-esteem? Or fear of hurting someone's feelings?

5. How would you tell a date that you're planning to date others? Write down how you would express this intention.

MEDITATION

Dateable: *Dating more than one person at a time allows me to refine my non-negotiables and build my self-confidence. I am grateful for the chance to date consciously, learning about myself and others.*

Mateable: *Dating more than one person at a time allows me the space to consciously, slowly, and wisely find a partner that supports who I am and shares my life visions. I know that he/she is waiting for me.*

Soul Dating Step 12:
Sex

If you're a mateable person who aspires to find your companion or soul mate, sex early in your dating relationship can be a major barrier to achieving your goal. Unfortunately, most people find it easier to be sexual than to be intimate, and we see many men and women sacrificing the deep intimacy that comes with a soul relationship for instant sexual gratification.

27

In the heat of lust, people often assume that intimacy, trust, and loyalty are present or will soon follow. Under the sway of romantic illusion, people believe that if they sleep with someone, these emotional bonds will naturally form. In fact, true friendship rarely develops when infatuation and passion dominate the relationship from the beginning.

When sex happens early in the dating process, it dramatically changes the nature of a relationship. The notion of being under a spell suggests how sex causes us to lose our natural objectivity and perceptivity. When sex comes too soon, it's very difficult to follow our soul dating steps: interviewing, being conscious of nonnegotiables, and keeping romantic illusion at bay. Sometimes, we're so needy and our self-esteem is so low that the driving force in our lives becomes making a connection through sex.

If you're dateable, of course, you don't have to wait to have sex (although you may choose to). You're dating to have fun rather than to establish a long-term relationship, and sex is nothing if not fun. As long as you take precautions against STDs and pregnancy, having sex is OK.

Mateable people are looking for more than fun. However, this talk of postponing sex may sound difficult if not impossible. It raises scores of issues that everyone struggles with. A better understanding of the issues involved will reduce the intensity of that struggle.

First, let's begin with this ground rule:

∽

Consciously choose to add sex to the relationship only when you know another person intimately and have developed a romantic friendship.

Typically, it takes about three to six months of seeing someone before you discover who the person really is and decide if both of you want to see each other exclusively. This doesn't mean that your dates during these first months have to take place in a puritanical atmosphere. There are many ways to be romantic and show affection that don't involve sex. The key is to maintain a balance in your behavior—even making out at home can be dicey, because it may become difficult to show restraint. Try to avoid putting yourself in compromising situations—going away together for a weekend, drinking too much, and so on.

What might help you avoid having sex too early in a relationship is recognizing how important it is to get to know another person slowly and develop compatibility and romantic friendship.

When Jennifer met Stuart she was immediately drawn to his gentle, warm manner. During the next three months they saw each other on a very regular basis. Jennifer became very optimistic about their future together because Stuart demonstrated many of her nonnegotiables. He knew exactly how to use his sense of humor to counter her serious nature; his outgoing, sensitive way was reflected in the many charity boards he sat on; and his successful law practice gave him the opportunity to travel regularly to Europe.

Almost from the start, Stuart suggested that sex be a part of their relationship. When Jennifer said she preferred to wait until they got to know each other better, he reluctantly went along.

It was after the three-month mark that Stuart's temper and erratic behavior started revealing itself. Jennifer felt dumbfounded, extremely disappointed, and very disillusioned.

"I'm so relieved I didn't sleep with him," she confided to her closest friend. "As hard as it's going to be to break up with Stuart now, just think how much harder it would be if we'd slept together. I would have been much more invested and emotionally attached."

We've had clients (especially women) tell us that premature sex sabotaged their relationships. Some who have had many sexual partners or serial monogamy talk about how sex was ultimately a shallow, meaningless experience without emotional intimacy. Your decision to add sex to the relationship should be conscious and the result of intimacy you've already established.

Mateable people reach a crossroads where they can add sex to a relationship. Though it would be convenient if this juncture always arose three to six months into the relationship, the time frame can vary. To help you determine when you've reached this point, here are some identifying traits:

◇ Both people like and love each other.
◇ You both know each other well enough to make the commitment to date each other exclusively.
◇ You're leading a balanced life.
◇ You're not in romantic illusion.
◇ Both of you know that you meet many of each other's nonnegotiables.
◇ You have developed a romantic friendship.
◇ You've experienced good and bad times together.
◇ You don't feel you have to "fix" the other person.
◇ You feel emotionally safe with each other.
◇ You have fun together.
◇ You discuss birth control, safe sex, sexual histories, and expectations for the relationship.
◇ You embrace the principles of this book and live them in your relationship.

There are a number of practical considerations we should address at this point. A frequently asked question involves what to say during dating when the subject of sex arises. Here's one way of framing the issue that can be helpful:

"I'm not ready for sex yet. I need to develop a romantic friendship first. It's not because I don't find you attractive, interesting, or sexy, but I need to be more emo-

tionally connected with you first and know there's the possibility that we're building a committed relationship."

If someone keeps pushing for sex even after you've explained how you feel about it, this is a person who isn't particularly concerned about your needs or building a lasting relationship. This behavior identifies a dateable person, and, if nothing else, the conflict over sex helps you know the other person's status.

Another common concern is the typical three-to-six-month waiting period and whether it can be shortened. We've found that if two people have done their emotional and spiritual work, if they're good interviewers, if they're open and vulnerable and communicative with each other, then it's possible to shorten that period. Still, we don't want to make it seem like most people are this evolved and can have sex after a month or two. We also don't want to pretend that it's easy to refrain from sexual activity for a sustained period of time. As much as we can tell you to exercise, masturbate, or take cold showers, it still requires inner fortitude to resist sex. If you're a spiritual person or aspire to be one, however, you should know that abstaining can be a very spiritual act. Sexual fasting is a good way to clear your mind, become more open to divine energy, and become more aware of new creative possibilities.

While men and women can both have trouble dealing with sexual abstinence, women are especially vulnerable to falling off the wagon because they, more than men, bond through sex. This is due in part to a hormone called oxytocin (the love hormone) that triggers orgasm. Because of oxytocin, women's bodies say "I'm in love" after having sex, even though their brains tell them, "You barely know this man." For some women, love becomes an addiction. Men are usually better able to stay uncommitted after sex.

Are there any exceptions to the rule that mateable people should wait? There are a few situations where sex may not jeopardize achievement of a companion or soul mate relationship. Sue, for instance, was dating two men and Joe seemed more right than the other man. Though Sue didn't know enough about Joe to commit to an exclusive relationship, she still had sex with him. The questions for Sue are: Can she still consciously and objectively interview Joe about her nonnegotiables? Can she avoid putting demands on him? How will she feel if he starts dating someone else? Will she agree that they only have sex with each other but can date others?

If Joe and Sue are honest with each other about all these questions, it's possible that they can continue to move the friendship to a mateable relationship. But as you can see, the development of the relationship becomes more complex with the introduction of sex before important issues have been resolved.

Both dateable and mateable people should have a pre-sex discussion about their post-sex expectations of the relationship. After sex is added, unrealistic expectations often arise. One person expects the other to call every night, to lock in every Saturday night for a date, or to never sleep with anyone else. By talking about what expectations each person has of the other before sex is added, many problems can be avoided.

SOUL DATEWORK

Sex can be wonderful but it's important to carefully explore your expectations before sleeping with your date.

1. Examine your beliefs about sex. Do they come from old messages that you got from your parents, church, friends, and society? Do you still value these beliefs or has your attitude shifted?

2. What are your motives for having sex? For a physical release, to tie someone to you, to create (false) intimacy, or to add another dimension to a well-developed romantic friendship (after six months)?

3. Think about a relationship in which you had great, passionate sex right from the start. Create a list of traits you would have used to describe this relationship in those early weeks. Create another list of traits that you would use to describe the relationship six months later (or close to the time when it was ending). If the two lists are different, how do you account for the difference? Did he or she change? Or did your perception of the relationship change, and if so, how and why?

4. If you do have sex early in the relationship, can you stay conscious and continue to interview?

5. Regardless of whether you're dateable or mateable, do you have frank discussions with your potential sexual partner(s), before sex, about blood tests, safe sex, expectations, etc.?

MEDITATION

Dateable: *I love myself enough to practice safe sex. No one will pressure me to do otherwise. I am at peace with my decision.*

Mateable: *I am willing to abstain from sex until I find the person who has the possibility of becoming my companion or soul mate. I rejoice in my choice to wait.*

Soul Dating Step 13: Creating a Marketing Plan

Now that you have developed a new attitude and have learned the skills to help you find a partner, it's time to create and implement a strategy, or marketing plan, to obtain the desired results. This plan depends on the relationship level you're seeking.

If a companion relationship is what you want, you need to devise a plan that focuses on doing activities—everything from cooking classes to wine tastings to tennis. Concentrating on outer-directed, intellectually stimulating activities that involve personality qualities will lead you to like-minded people who share similar values and perspectives.

On the other hand, if you're looking for a soul mate or spiritual partner relationship, you'd naturally look for activities or places where you'd be likely to make more soulful connections. This might include spiritual workshops or classes, retreats, Sierra Club meetings, yoga classes, etc. People choose these activities for two reasons. One is to connect with like-minded individuals who value a more intimate psychological and spiritual interaction. The second is to help them continue on their path of personal growth.

Individuals looking for soul mates or spiritual partners have a keen desire to go places and do things where there's a significant amount of sharing and feeling; they want to engage in activities where they're being touched emotionally, psychologically, and spiritually. Even when they're doing things like going to a party or a sports event, they're highly conscious of showing up authentically, desiring a more nurturing, heartfelt dialogue. They want to impact others on more than a personality level.

While those who will enter into spiritual partnerships are also looking to make soulful connections, they attend functions and join activities in order to keep learning and growing. Their plan is ultimately directed by the universe, because a higher power is responsible for bringing them together.

No matter which of the three levels you aspire to, the soul dating steps direct and support this process. Either you have incorporated them into the way you're creating your plan or you're working at doing so. The important thing is to declare your commitment to the process.

❧

The moment one definitely commits oneself then Providence moves to us . . . all sorts of things occur to help one that would never otherwise have occurred. A whole stream of events issues from the decision, raising in one's favor all manner of unforeseen incidents and meetings and material assistance, which no man could have dreamt would come his way.

—W. H. Murray (discussing his expedition
to the summit of Mt. Everest)

❧

As this quotation suggests, once you make a conscious decision to date in order to find a spiritual partner, soul mate, or companion, you experience the same unexplainable assistance in your search as Murray describes. The more committed you are to finding your appropriate partner, the more likely that you'll discover that individual. The more time you spend, the more psychospiritual work you do, and the greater focus you have, the more likely that person will come into your life.

Marketing yourself is nothing less than making a commitment to yourself that you'll do things, choose places, and perform the necessary inner work that supports who you want to be. This means being open to the possibilities all around you—the specific places, situations, and environments where you might meet your companion or soul mate—and selectively capitalizing on them. If you're approachable and take advantage of the interviewing process, just about any activity or location is a possibility for meeting your partner if you bring your most authentic self. You increase the odds of finding that partner if you choose places most likely to attract people who share your values.

It's not only your relationship level that affects your marketing but your mateable/dateable status. Dateable people are out there doing a lot of practicing and socializing. They're practicing being approachable, getting clarity on their nonnegotiables, interviewing, having fun, and developing the skills to be mateable. Mateable people, on the other hand, are focusing on meeting appropriate people and identifying who's not appropriate.

As a result of these two different goals, people need to be clear about how to market themselves based on their mateable/dateable status. Let's look at the differences in approach in three common dating environments:

Bars. This is a tool for dateable people, since meetings in bars tend to be based on outer rather than inner qualities. It's very difficult to interview at a bar; it's hard to get beneath the surface because of the noise, distractions, and expectations that come with a bar encounter. For dateable people bars provide good opportunities to practice approachable skills and flirting. This isn't an easy or appropriate place to find a soul mate.

Personal Ads. These ads can be written in dateable or mateable ways. They also can be written to attract a companion or soul mate. The mateable content should revolve around nonnegotiables and communicate a highly authentic, mateable message. The dateable content is light, surface-oriented (appearance, hobbies, etc.), and fun-focused.

The following are examples of dateable and mateable ads:

Dateable: *SWM, 34, 5'7", good-looking, professional, and independent, looking for some fun in the sun. Enjoys all types of water sports, cycling, tennis, cultural events, cooking together, ethnic dining and travel. Seeking a great-looking SWF, 28–35, warm, physically fit, who has similar interests. No dependents.*

Mateable (soul mate/spiritual partner): *By describing who I want, you'll have a good sense of who I am: DWF, 5'7", 45, smart, spirited, good-looking, Christian redhead asking for a 40–50-year-old man of integrity who's confident, financially stable, fit. He believes in family values, understands/appreciates the differences in the sexes, has close relationships with family/friends and takes special care of those he loves. He understands his past, wants to share emotional intimacies, nature, spirituality and communicate at a soul level. He loves and celebrates us as the perfectly flawed individuals that we are.*

Fix-Ups and Dating Services. Dateable people don't have to be particularly detailed or discriminating in describing the type of people they want to go out with. Beyond wanting someone whom they find fun and attractive, they can play the field. Mateable people, however, need to be very specific about the qualities they're looking for, based on their nonnegotiables. They should never assume that others know who and what they're looking for.

SOUL DATEWORK

If you want to get what you are looking for, you need to present yourself to the world in such a way that it will be reflected back to you.

1. As a dateable person, do you have a well-thought-out marketing plan that generates dating opportunities? Does the strategy help you practice being approachable and refine your nonnegotiable list? Does it help you move from dateable to mateable? If you don't have a plan and find yourself resisting creating one, identify the reason why you're blocked. Is it inertia? Self-esteem issues? Laziness? Negative self-talk?

2. Before you can market yourself as the kind of person looking for a companion or soul mate relationship, answer this question: "Am I the kind of companion/soul mate who would attract the kind of companion/soul mate I'm looking for?"

3. As someone looking for a companion relationship, does your marketing approach mirror the values and activities that would attract your companion?

4. As a person looking for a soul mate relationship, does your marketing strategy reflect the more soulful connections, emotional intimacy, and personal growth that you need to attract your soul mate?

MEDITATION

Dateable: *I am dating to learn more about myself and others and to become a more successful dater. By being proactive and creating a marketing blueprint, I am helping myself realize that goal.*

Mateable: *I am committed to creating a plan that will direct me to meeting the companion or soul mate I desire and deserve. Until then, I will date to learn more about myself and others.*

Soul Dating Step 14:
Is This the One?

There comes a pivotal moment in soul dating when we are ready to decide if we're going to stop dating others and start seeing one person exclusively. Most people usually mark this event by getting engaged and planning the wedding. They don't recognize that there is a middle step—asking the question, Is this the one? Asking presents the opportunity to get to know the other person and let him or her know you at an even deeper level to determine if you are, indeed, life partners.

While it's possible that getting to know someone at this level will convince you that he or she is not the one, it's also possible that you'll discover that you've found your companion or soul mate. This is a two-part process.

EXCLUSIVITY

How do you know when you should stop dating others? There's no rule of thumb that says it's time; you can't arbitrarily say that after twenty dates, you should make it an exclusive relationship. When you reach a point where you've decided to be exclusive and are attempting to create the we, you must have integrated the following criteria:

⬧ You've gotten past the lust and really like and love someone for who he or she is.

⬧ You're clear about your nonnegotiables and what you value in a relationship.

⬥ You've dated enough that you trust yourself to choose a partner with the qualities that support and reflect your nonnegotiables.

⬥ You've interviewed this person enough to know that he or she is mate-able and appears to possess qualities that indicate he or she desires to be in and is capable of a companion or soul mate relationship.

⬥ You feel the other person is emotionally safe.

⬥ You choose to be with this person because he or she adds to your full, balanced life.

⬥ You've experienced anger and communication breakdowns and have been able to work through them.

⬥ You're able to ask the other person for what you want and can graciously accept an occasional no.

⬥ You also feel free to say no, but more often say yes.

⬥ You think about the other person's needs without losing touch with your own.

For people seeking a soul mate or spiritual partner:

⬥ You're using multisensory information, relying on your intuition and higher self to know that it's time to be exclusive.

⬥ You've assessed that your partner has done enough emotional, psychological, and spiritual work.

⬥ Your partner encourages you to grow and attain higher goals and you do the same for him or her.

SOUL DATEWORK

1. To help determine if you're ready to move from dating others to an exclusive relationship, answer the following questions:

◇ How would you feel if you didn't leave the door open for other possible dating relationships?

◇ Would you be scared to "give up your freedom"?

◇ Would you feel that by giving your time and emotions to only one person you'd be "trapped" or enmeshed in the relationship?

◇ Could you maintain your personal space and boundaries if you stop dating others?

◇ Are you deciding to date this one individual because you feel like it's the best you can do, that you have no other options and are willing to settle?

◇ Are you making this decision because you're needy or because you feel it's right?

2. Now imagine if this person were no longer in your life. How do you feel—sad, relieved, etc.? Would you miss how he or she contributes to your life? Is it easy or difficult to conceive of a future that doesn't include him or her?

3. Go back and look over our definition of romantic friendship on page 104. Does your relationship with this person meet that definition? Create a list of romantic friendship traits that characterize your relationship.

MEDITATION

I've reached a juncture in my life where I'm ready to stop dating others and start seeing this one person exclusively.

INVENTING THE WE

Now that you've decided to be a we, it's time to discover if this will be a lifetime partnership. While inventing your relationship, you need to investigate the following questions:

◇ Who am I and what am I committed to?
◇ What is my partner committed to?

⬧ What kind of we do I want and what kind of we does my partner want?

⬧ Are we capable of achieving this we together?

When you make the commitment to date only each other, you continue inventing the we together. This process involves talking about what you want your relationship to look like and doing the work together to make that type of relationship happen.

As the relationship moves deeper, shadow parts of each person surface, and you need to be prepared to confront them honestly and openly. Clear and authentic communication is crucial here. Working on the we of a relationship is a time to further clarify your nonnegotiables, make requests, set limits, state opinions and feelings, disagree, apologize, forgive, and give up the need to be right.

As you date one person exclusively, you may find issues surfacing that may be impossible to resolve. For instance, Bart and Gretta have dated for six months, the last two exclusively. From the very beginning, Gretta was aware that Bart had a different work ethic and outlook concerning money. Gretta assumed that the friendship between them would help both reach a satisfactory compromise. But when they stopped seeing other people, money issues became a major bone of contention and produced name-calling and hostility. Gretta felt Bart was lazy and a spendthrift, while Bart told Gretta she was uptight and unrealistic about both work and money. The intensity of seeing each other exclusively brought these issues into the open, and it's quite possible that if they are unresolvable, Gretta and Bart should break up.

SOUL DATEWORK

As you're inventing the we, the following concerns and questions might arise. As you read them, consider whether you and your partner can work them through:

⬧ How do we spend our time alone and together?

⬧ What are some of the fears and issues that come up as we ponder being together forever?

◇ Can we help each other learn and grow?

◇ What can we do together to make our community a better place?

◇ What inner work do we have to continue that will impact on the relationship?

◇ Can we maintain consistent, low-level passion and romance both in and out of the bedroom?

◇ How do we improve our ability to work through power struggles and argue fairly?

◇ Can we give up the need to be right and commit ourselves to a win-win situation by apologizing and forgiving?

As you continue to invent the we, add your own issues and concerns to this list.

MEDITATION

We are committed to the process of consciously creating the we to determine if we will be lifelong partners.

Spiritual
Partnership

V

The Ultimate Connection

Spiritual partnership is a lifetime relationship level to which we can all aspire. Partners find each other because they're being rewarded for doing their emotional, psychological, and spiritual work. Some spiritual partners acknowledge that if they hadn't met their partner, they would have chosen to be alone, without a partner, for the rest of their lives.

Some had earlier passed on the opportunity to marry their soul mate in order to hold out for their spiritual partner. They listened to their inner voice that told them to wait and be patient. Other spiritual partners took a different route, through soul mate relationships and marriage, and arrived at the same point, ready for a deeper spiritual connection. In order for a couple to elevate from soul mate to spiritual partnership, both must do their individual work and value this type of transcendent relationship.

When spiritual partners are together, it feels magical. Synchronicity is another way of describing the amazing harmony of the partners. They have reached the point where they don't have to spend time making the relationship work. Because it functions so well, they can work on deeper personal issues. This kind of partnership is so strong, it doesn't require other people around it to give it life. It is complete and self-sustaining in the best sense. The partners value the purity of the relationship and find it to be the one place where they feel completely safe.

There is tremendous reassurance, comfort, and serenity in this partnership which encourages each partner to say or work on anything without fear of blame, shame, or judgment. This type of union is visionary: seeing abundance and prosperity where other relationships see scarcity. Spiritual partners understand that everything happens for a reason and are at peace, knowing that they can contend with whatever life presents.

Because it happens through divine intervention, spiritual partners cannot control when it occurs; thus, they often meet in unexpected and unusual ways. When they are brought together, their souls instantly unite. The feeling is transcendent. From the first meeting, spiritual partners feel and talk as if they've known each other forever and are simply filling each other in like old friends who have been reunited. People often tell us about a series of magical and mysterious events that brought their spiritual partners to them—events that can't be explained logically.

Here is the story of the preparation that both Basha and Jeff did in order to be ready for their remarkable meeting. We'll hear from Jeff first.

I was married to Bunny for sixteen years. In February 1993, she was diagnosed with stage four breast cancer and the doctors gave her six months to live. This devastating news came in the wake of a series of recent tragedies in my life, including the deaths of both my in-laws and the loss of several other close family members. I couldn't accept the loss of my wife and convinced her to undergo some radical chemotherapy, even though she was initially opposed.

That June, I resigned my position as an elementary school principal to care for her. I took her for chemotherapy and radiation several times a week. She fought valiantly for a while and her condition improved. When she stabilized, during the summer, we decided that I would return to work on a part-time basis.

At this part-time job, I met Howie, who instantly became a pivotal person in my life. I'm sure that the universe put us together precisely at this time. I'm convinced he was God's messenger, sent to help me understand what was occurring and guiding me along my spiritual path. In September, my father entered the hospital with lung problems and died within two months.

During this awful time, there was a remarkable grace in Bunny's and my relationship as we prepared for her death. The lessons I learned from Bunny and the magnificence with which she handled her death intimately changed who I was and what I have become. Over the years, we had shared a soul mate relationship and I grew immensely during this partnership. She taught me, by her example, how to face both life and death with dignity and to embrace my spirituality in a way I never imagined.

After Bunny's death, I spent many hours in solitude pondering my existence and finally came to peace with all that had happened. During this time, Howie was always there, guiding me through these muddy waters. Those six months were truly my Dark Night of the Soul. I came out, on the other end, emotionally healed and ready to resume my life. This spiritual journey was both a culmination and a new beginning. My life's perspective changed as I watched the logical, scientific Jeff, whom I knew so well, metamorphose into a feeling and truly intuitive being.

Howie and his wife, Diana, always tried to include me in their activities. As a matter of fact, Diana was one of my dating coaches, as I had not dated in over eighteen years. One evening, they introduced me to Carol, one of Howie's closest childhood friends. Carol's husband, Don, was playing piano at a jazz club in New Jersey. That evening, as Don was playing, Carol and I connected above the noise and spoke intimately for several hours on a wide range of subjects, mostly focusing on my losses and new life. Miraculously, I was able to talk and listen in this atmosphere in spite of being overly sensitive to sound. Something allowed Carol's voice to be heard and we were able to communicate intimately.

At the end of the evening, Carol said to me, "I have never done anything like this before, but I have the perfect woman for you."

"Fine, tell me about her."

Carol proceeded to tell me about her friend Basha, who was a successful clinical psychologist living in Chicago. I started laughing and told her, "Wait a minute, I'm not prepared to get on a plane now and go to Chicago."

"Don't worry about it," Carol responded. "Basha would be happy to come to New York to meet you."

"What if we connect? I'm not prepared to leave New York now, since I have just dealt with all these losses."

"Don't worry. Basha will give up her practice and life in Chicago and come here to be with you."

I was later to find out that she had no earthly way of knowing this information, as she and Basha only talked on occasion. In fact, I came to realize that the information Carol was sharing had to be mystical, channeled to her from some universal energy, because that's exactly what happened.

I told her to let me know when Basha would be in town and we ended the evening. The next day (Carol lets no grass grow under her feet), she called and told me that Basha would be coming to New Jersey on Saturday, April eighth, and would stay at her house for three days. I don't know what possessed me to set aside three days to meet some person who didn't meet my external picture of a potential partner (my personality nonnegotiables). Carol was introducing me to a Jewish woman who was my age. I was looking for a younger, non-Jewish woman. Surprisingly, I didn't follow my head, but trusted some inner voice. I entered "Basha Weekend" on my calendar and made no other commitments except playing golf. This was very unlike me, especially considering the messenger and the message.

I left for a month in Florida, where I enjoyed being alone, reflecting on my life. Then, April eighth came. I decided to drive alone to New Jersey, just in case Basha and I connected and I needed to be independent. I followed Howie and Diana to Carol's house and we arrived at 7:30 for dinner. When the door opened I asked, "Where's Basha?"

"She's feeling sick; she just threw up, but she'll be out by eight."

Some introduction! Anyway, at eight P.M., Basha walked down the hallway and the most incredible feeling came over me. I couldn't focus on what she looked like. Instead, I felt this warmth, this glow that invaded my being. She came down the stairs with a shiny red nose and all I saw was white and yellow light. I didn't see any of her physical characteristics. It was as if I was looking directly through her eyes, into her soul. I didn't understand what was happening but I knew this was different from anything I had ever felt before.

Now Basha tells what she was experiencing:

I met Carol twenty years ago in California, where we were both studying for our doctorates in clinical psychology. We became friends during that time and maintained a sisterlike relationship over the years, even though our lives took different paths. She married and within fifteen years had four children and decided that her calling was to become an Orthodox Jew. We remained in touch by talking to each other a few times each year.

Carol called me during January 1995, several months after my father died, at a time when I had no interest in developing any type of relationship. She told me about Jeff and insisted that I come to New York to meet him. My life felt overwhelming. My father had just died suddenly and my mom was ill. I was busy caring for her, going through my own healing process, and, at the same time, continued to see clients. Many nights I would go to sleep crying and asking God to support me *because I felt that I couldn't handle my life. I knew intuitively that he would only be giving me what I could handle so I just prayed that I could get through each day. Any free time I had, I spent praying, journaling, and going to workshops, including, in February, a workshop that Caroline Myss gave in Mexico. I felt so overextended and depleted that I had no interest in meeting a man. Initially, I said to Carol that this was not the right time for me to meet Jeff. Carol, who normally is quite verbose, immediately countered with two succinct statements that I couldn't refute:*

⬦ *"Jeff stopped working to take care of his wife who was dying of cancer." (After much soulwork, I value the importance of being with someone who would be with me in the good and bad times.)*

⬦ *"Basha, you talk about being mateable, but you don't know how to be married. Jeff does. He's different from all the other men you dated who wanted you to take care of them. Jeff will be there for you and he understands how to be in a partnership. He knows how to be married. If you're serious about getting married, you have to meet this man."*

Hearing this, I had no choice. I couldn't dispute anything she said and even though it didn't feel like the right time, I agreed to meet Jeff. The first available date for both of us was Saturday, April eighth. That morning I woke up feeling very ill. I was very sick but I couldn't cancel the trip because it was Saturday, the Jewish Sabbath, and Carol wouldn't answer the phone. Since she had arranged for someone to pick me up at the airport, I had to go. I would have done anything to cancel because looking good was very important to me and I don't feel very lovable and attractive when I'm sick. As I sat on the plane, I was laughing to myself as I said, "God, there must be some reason why I am meeting this wonderful man and I am going there sick."

I arrived late in the afternoon and Carol immediately realized I was ill. She took my temperature and discovered that I had a 102-degree fever. She filled me up with the herbs echinacea and goldenseal and I went to bed for a few hours until Jeff was to arrive. Even though I was exhausted, I tried to dress up and look as good as I could. I walked down the hall and saw him. He was cute!

We all sat in the living room and made small talk. As I usually do, I shared my feelings and told him I thought he was cute. He didn't respond so I figured that he didn't find me attractive. We then got onto the subject of Jeff's dating experiences over the past few months. He said that he was being fixed up by everyone, sometimes dating two or three women in one week. From these experiences, he related that he couldn't necessarily decide if he liked a woman right away; however, he knew immediately if there was no possibility, no chemistry. I assumed by this comment that Jeff was giving me a hint that he didn't find me attractive, and I quickly stated, "Men are all shallow." There was some laughter and Jeff looked at me with a warm smile, easing my trepidation a bit. At the same time, I told myself that I needed to be with someone who would like me in the bad as well as the good times. Although I felt sad, I was O.K. with it. (The next day I found out that the reason he didn't respond when I said that he was cute was because he was shy, not because he didn't find me attractive.)

We all sat down to dinner. Immediately, I felt so sick that I excused myself and sat down on a chair in the living room. Within a few minutes, Jeff asked if there was anything he could do. I somehow listened to my inner voice, remembering that I needed to interview for inner qualities, so I replied, "T.L.C.—tender loving care." He got up from the table, sat on the edge of my chair, and kissed me on the forehead. In front of the chair was a glass table, and as soon as he kissed my forehead, his leg shot up and smashed into it. Howie, viewing this, immediately said, "It's all over. You two are meant for each other." We both laughed. I was feeling so sick; all I wanted to do was to get into bed. Jeff said that he would like to see me tomorrow if I felt better.

The next day, even though I was still feeling ill, Carol told me I had to call Jeff; she wouldn't take no for an answer. I reluctantly called Jeff and we decided that the four of us would go to dinner. (Jeff related that he spent Sunday morning at home, reading the New York Times, *waiting impatiently for a call from me. If I hadn't called, he said he would have accepted it, as he was at a point in his life where he felt the universe would decide his fate. He was, however, relieved when I called.)*

That evening, the four of us went to a kosher Chinese restaurant in Teaneck, New Jersey. I had begun to feel better and suddenly noticed this powerful energy between Jeff and me, a warm glow filling me up. As we sat in the restaurant, we were subtly touching each other. It was like something beyond the physical, an energetic attraction or light caressing both of us. The chemistry was remarkable! It was as if we were there together and always had been. The conversation we had was revealing and completely intimate and being together felt totally natural.

We returned to Carol and Don's and went into the library to be alone for the first time. We continued to share intimately, slowly leaning in to each other. After about two hours, I finally kissed him. When our lips met, our souls merged and I felt this transcendent experience, a warm glow of golden light surrounding us. Miraculously, I kept feeling better and better. He was giving me hints that he found me attractive and there was something about the way we were together that just felt right.

Suddenly, I was able to see his soul. He had touched my essence in a way that no one had before. The night before, I knew there was something special, but, feeling so sick, I couldn't trust it. After Jeff left, I couldn't sleep. I couldn't wait to see him the next day and was disappointed that he was playing golf in the morning. He asked what I would like to do, maybe go to dinner, and I answered, "No, I want to go hiking with you in the woods because we both like the outdoors, and I want to see your house in Westchester. I want to see where you live. A house tells a lot about a person and we could have dinner anytime."

Initially, I only had the weekend to get to know him, since I was returning to Chicago on Tuesday afternoon. Our focus was on bonding, intimacy, and honest communication. There was no game-playing or small talk. We had fun while we were getting to know each other. After the walk, we brought in food and went to his house. We had dinner, I met his cat, Isis, and I toured his house. As we continued to reveal ourselves to each other, the passion and connection grew. I soon realized that what I was experiencing with Jeff was on an entirely different level.

As we hugged and kissed, we asked each other very direct and critical questions. He asked me why I was never married, because he thought I was so wonderful and couldn't understand how I could remain unattached all my life. I asked him detailed questions about his relationship with his late wife, because I wanted to make sure that I didn't get into a dysfunctional relationship since I had worked so hard to heal myself. We were open and not at all defensive. Truth was paramount. We both let our hair down and bared our souls to each other. Somehow we knew we were in safe hands, with God directing behind the scenes, a true spiritual partnership. He saw me at my worst and loved me for it. That must be the reason that I was sick coming to New York because I needed to really believe that someone could love me with all my imperfections.

I found out that this was also very special for Jeff. He had been dating quite a bit for several months but had never gone beyond kissing. It was as if we had done several months of interviewing in one evening. This was the most loving and intimate experience we both ever had and the intensity was beyond anything we ever felt.

Since I was leaving the next day, we decided that we would continue to learn about each other by telephone until Jeff came to visit me in Chicago ten days later. During this time, we spoke each evening, learning more intimate details as we continued to reveal ourselves.

Finally, the day came when I was to pick Jeff up at the airport. We were both very excited and anxious about seeing each other. Unbelievably, we later discovered that we were both concerned that we would not recognize each other because we had

connected on a different, almost transcendent level. In fact, Jeff related that he was-
n't sure he would even know who I was physically. He knew my soul but could not
remember my face. I realized that I felt the same way. What a relief it was when we
finally faced each other at the airport and reconnected on the physical level as well.

We were married six months later on October 1, 1995. The most amazing part
of our relationship is how easy and smooth it has been and we feel more connected
each day.

If you aspire to spiritual partnership, the following is a list of attributes,
present in Basha and Jeff's story, that are necessary before you can find your
spiritual partner:

◇ They have done their own psychospiritual work.
◇ They value who qualities rather than what qualities in themselves and
  their partner.
◇ They value consciousness and refuse to live in illusion.
◇ Their soul and personality are aligned.
◇ They value meaningfulness and contribution in their lives.
◇ They have attained a balanced, full life.
◇ They are able to use multiple perspectives.
◇ They know who they are and are very clear about the kind of person
  who would support them.
◇ They show up authentically, valuing intimacy and communication.
◇ They have a strong connection to their higher self and the universe.
◇ They trust that the divine will bring them their partner when they are
  ready.
◇ They regard their intuition and feelings as more important than their
  logic and five senses when communicating with each other.

The following are the elements that make up a spiritual partnership:

◇ They know each other so well that there are no surprises.
◇ They have no power struggles because they value cooperation rather
  than competition.
◇ They deal with issues, rather than solutions.

⋄ They are very aware of their past history and support each other in the healing process.
⋄ They are committed for their lifetime to help each other learn and grow.
⋄ Their contribution to others is a major goal of the relationship.
⋄ They value unconditional love and are committed to mutual support.

SOUL DATEWORK

Individuals on this journey toward spiritual partnership prepare themselves in all sorts of ways—being on the path, entering the Dark Night of the Soul, learning to love themselves unconditionally—for the moment when the divine would bring them their partner.

For individuals seeking a spiritual partner, one way of attracting that kind of soulful connection is to write a letter to God describing in detail what you're looking for in your partner and asking God to bring this person to you when you're ready. You are now asking multisensory, divine energy to assist you in your search.

Prepare a detailed and intimate picture of the person you desire, using your nonnegotiables and coming from your heart and inner voice. To help you with this exercise, here are two letters Basha wrote in her journal to God after she ended a four-year soul mate relationship. Fourteen months later she met Jeff, who, amazingly, matched all the attributes Basha desired.

2/17/94
Dear God,

I am ready to love completely and enter a spiritual partnership that leads to marriage. I want a man who is as loving as I am and wants a romantic friendship—not love at first sight. Someone who adores and cherishes me. That cares about making me happy. I want someone who is generous with me. Who values friendship, sharing, freedom and spirituality. Who is beautiful both inside and out. Who values nature, travel and learning. Who's affectionate and caring. Who is not afraid of my ability to love so deeply. Is thrilled about my successes, not intimidated. He values a healthy lifestyle and wants to share with me as well as give me space—encouraging me to grow and learn (vice versa). He values open communication and lovingness *above* all. He's committed to personal and spiritual growth. Loves nature and animals. Is positive about life. Is spiritual—not religious. Is open to trying new things. Is somewhat materialistic but above all values spirituality. Is bright, college-educated, preferably Jewish, blue eyes with dimples and a bright, big, warm smile. I also need a man of courage, a warrior who is willing to embrace love and life fully and does not choose safety and sameness. Someone who lives on the edge.

Love, Basha

6/15/94

Dear God,

I totally surrender to you. I realize that I don't know how to pick someone who isn't like Jake [my father], and can't appreciate me and give me what I want and need. My antenna only goes for that type. I beat myself up and suffer. You're in charge now. I love you. You are in charge of all areas now. Please let me know how much work I should do as part of surrendering to you. I need all your help and support in trusting your timing in this process.

Love, Basha

MEDITATION

I am committed to do whatever work is necessary and to wait patiently until divine intervention directs me to a spiritual union. I am content to remain alone until we are both ready.

A Final Word

Congratulations! We are proud of you for completing this courageous and illuminating journey of self-exploration and discovery. We are confident that this path has led to magnificent breakthroughs that have helped to heal your mind, body, and spirit.

As so many of our clients have expressed and we hope you have learned, our soul dating process has made you a wiser and empowered participant in your dating and relationship life. As one of our workshop participants so aptly put it, "This journey has been as important as my original destination—finding a soul mate."

We believe that finding and developing a soul mate relationship is within everyone's reach. By living the Seven Spiritual Wisdoms and completing the soulwork and soul dating steps, we are confident you will reap the reward by finding your life partner. Then, together, you will continue the quest for personal growth and spiritual fulfillment both as an individual and as a partner.

Selected Bibliography

Albom, Mitch. *Tuesdays with Morrie*. New York: Doubleday, 1997.

Allen, Patricia, and Sandra Harmon. *Getting to "I Do."* New York: Avon Books, 1994.

Bloomfield, Harold. *Love Secrets for a Lasting Relationship*. New York: Bantam Books, 1992.

Branden, Nathaniel. *How to Raise Your Self-Esteem*. New York: Bantam Books, 1988.

Breathnach, Sarah Ban. *Simple Abundance*. New York: Warner Books, 1995.

Cameron, Julia. *The Artist's Way*. New York: G. P. Putnam's Sons, 1992.

Carlson, Richard, and Benjamin Shield, eds. *Healers on Healing*. Los Angeles: Jeremy Tarcher, 1989.

Chapman, Gary. *The Five Love Languages*. Chicago: Northfield Publishing, 1995.

Chopra, Deepak. *The Path to Love*. New York: Harmony Books, 1997.

Colgrove, Melba, Harold Bloomfield, and Peter McWilliams. *How to Survive the Loss of a Love*. New York: Leo Press, 1976.

De Angelis, Barbara. *Are You the One for Me?* New York: Delacorte Press, 1992.

De Mello, Anthony. *Sadhana, a Way to God*. New York: Doubleday, 1978.

Dyer, Wayne W. *Real Magic*. New York: HarperCollins, 1992.

———. *Your Sacred Self*. New York: HarperCollins, 1995.

Fast, Julius. *Body Language*. New York: Pocket Books, 1971.

Gray, John. *Men Are from Mars, Women Are from Venus*. New York: Harper-Collins, 1992.

Hoff, Benjamin. *The Tao of Pooh*. New York: Penguin Books, 1982.

Joudry, Patricia, and Maurie Pressman. *Twin Souls*. New York: Carol Southern Books, 1993.

Katz, Stan, and Aimee Liu. *False Love and Other Romantic Illusions*. New York: Pocket Books, 1988.

Kingman, Daphne Rose. *Finding True Love*. Berkeley: Conari Press, 1996.

Kushner, Harold. *Who Needs God*. New York: Summit Books, 1989.

Leonard, Linda. *On the Way to the Wedding*. Boston: Shambhala, 1987.

Louden, Jennifer. *The Woman's Comfort Book*. San Francisco: HarperSanFrancisco, 1992.

Moody, Harry. *The Five Stages of the Soul*. New York: Anchor Books, 1997.

Myss, Caroline. *Anatomy of the Spirit*. New York: Harmony Books, 1996.

Newton, Michael. *Journey of Souls*. St. Paul, Minn.: Llewellyn Publications, 1997.

Orloff, Judith. *Second Sight*. New York: Warner Books, 1996.

Peck, M. Scott. *The Road Less Traveled*. New York: Touchstone Books, 1978.

Redfield, James. *The Celestine Prophecy*. New York: Warner Books, 1993.

Remen, Rachel Naomi. *Kitchen Table Wisdom*. New York: Riverhead Books, 1996.

Rinpoche, Sogyal. *The Tibetan Book of Living and Dying*. San Francisco: HarperSanFrancisco, 1992.

Roane, Susan. *How to Work a Room*. New York: Warner Books, 1988.

Shealy, C. Norman. *The Self-Healing Workbook*. Rockport, Mass: Element Books, 1993.

Sheehy, Gail. *New Passages*. New York: Ballatine Books, 1995.

Shield, Benjamin, and Richard Carlson, eds. *For the Love of God*. San Rafael, Calif.: New World Library, 1990.

Sills, Judith. *A Fine Romance*. Los Angeles: Jeremy Tarcher, 1987.

Vanzant, Iyanla. *One Day My Soul Just Opened Up*. New York: Fireside Books, 1998.

Wakefield, Dan. *The Story of Your Life*. Boston: Beacon Press, 1990.

Walsch, Neale Donald. *Conversations with God*. New York: G. P. Putnam's Sons, 1995.

Zukav, Gary. *The Seat of the Soul*. New York: Simon and Schuster, 1989.

Selected Audiotapes

Beattie, Melody. *Codependent No More: How to Stop Controlling Others and Start Caring for Yourself.* 1998.

———. *The Language of Letting Go.* 1998.

Bradshaw, John E. *Healing the Shame That Binds You* (2 cassettes). 1989.

———. *Bradshaw on the Family: A New Way of Creating Solid Self-Esteem.* 1989.

Brussat, Frederic. *Spiritual Literacy: Reading the Sacred in Everyday Life.* 1998.

Buscaglia, Leo. *Loving Each Other: The Challenge of Human Relationships.* 1995.

Carlson, Richard. *Don't Sweat the Small Stuff . . . And It's All Small Stuff.* 1997.

Chopra, Deepak. *Overcoming Addiction: The Spiritual Solution.* 1997.

Dass, Ram. *Spiritual Practices and Perspectives.* 1994.

De Angelis, Barbara. *Making Relationships Work* (2 cassettes). 1995.

———. *Ask Barbara: The 100 Most-Asked Questions about Love, Sex, and Relationships.* 1996.

Dyer, Wayne W. *Your Sacred Self* (2 cassettes). 1995.

———. *Manifest Your Destiny: The Nine Spiritual Principles for Getting Everything You Want* (2 cassettes). 1997.

Gawain, Shakti. *Relationships as Mirrors.* 1991.

Gray, John. *What You Feel, You Can Heal: A Guide for Enriching Relationships* (2 cassettes). 1995.

———. *Men Are from Mars, Women Are from Venus* (2 cassettes). 1996.

———. *Mars and Venus in Love* (2 cassettes). 1996.

———. *Mars and Venus on a Date.* 1997.

———. *Men, Women, and Relationships.* 1998.

———. *Mars and Venus Starting Over: A Practical Guide for Finding Love Again after a Painful Breakup, Divorce, or the Loss of a Loved One.* 1998.

Hay, Louise L. *I Love My Body.* 1991.

———. *You Can Heal Your Life.* 1996.

Hendrix, Harville. *Getting the Love You Want: A Guide for Couples.* 1989.

Kornfield, Jack. *The Heart of Spiritual Practice.* 1997.

Kreidman, Ellen. *The 10-Second Kiss.* 1998.

Moore, Thomas. *Meditations.* 1994.

———. *The Re-enchantment of Everyday Life* (2 cassettes). 1996.

———. *The Education of the Heart* (2 cassettes). 1996.

Moody, Harold, David Carroll, and Harry R. Moody. *The Five Stages of the Soul: Charting the Spiritual Passages That Shape Our Lives.* 1997.

Moran, Victoria. *A Shelter for the Spirit: How to Make Your Home a Haven in a Hectic World.* 1998.

Myss, Caroline. *Why People Don't Heal and How They Can.* 1995.

———. *Anatomy of the Spirit: The Seven Stages of Power and Healing.* 1996.

———. *Spiritual Madness.* 1997.

———. *Healing with Spirit.* 1997.

Nierenberg, Gerard I., and Henry H. Calero. *How to Read a Person like a Book.* 1985.

Riskas, Thomas. *Working Beneath the Surface: Attending to the Soul's "Hidden Agenda" for Wholeness, Fulfillment, and Deep Spiritual Healing.* 1998.

Robbins, Anthony, and John Gray. *Powertalk!: On Creating Extraordinary Relationships* (2 cassettes). 1996.

Schlessinger, Laura. *Ten Stupid Things Women Do to Mess Up Their Lives.* 1995.

———. *Ten Stupid Things Men Do to Mess Up Their Lives* (2 cassettes). 1997.

Tannen, Deborah. *That's Not What I Meant: How Conversational Style Makes or Breaks Relationships.* 1991.

True, Dan, Wendy Hall, Nicholas Coudsy, and Julie Schaller. *What Do Women Want from Men?* 1997.

Weil, Andrew, and Michael Toms. *The Roots of Healing.* 1997.

———. *Sound Body, Sound Mind: Music for Healing.* 1998.

Williamson, Marianne. *Marianne Williamson on Relationships.* 1992.

———. *The Marianne Williamson Relationships Workshop* (2 cassettes). 1993.

———. *Romantic Relationships* (4 cassettes). 1997.

———. *Positive Relationships.* 1998.

Zukav, Gary. *The Seat of the Soul.* 1991.

Zweig, Connie, and Steve Wolf. *Romancing the Shadow: A Guide to Transforming the Dark Side of Relationships.* 1997.

Index

Please Contact Us

Basha and Gail would like to hear from you. If you're interested in receiving information on our lectures and workshops or a forthcoming newsletter for singles, please visit our Web site

www.soulmating.com

or

write, enclosing a #10 self-addressed, stamped envelope, to:

Gail Prince
P.O. Box 464
Evanston, IL 60204